Best XI
Liverpool

Chris Bascombe, Nick Judd, Ben Lyttleton,
Leo Moynihan & Paul Tomkins

Publishing Information
Paperback edition, first published in December 2012 by Calm Publishing Ltd. United Kingdom Printed in UK. Marston Gate.

ISBN13: 978-0-9571291-5-3

Series editor: Paul Hansford

Cover design: Dane Gartrell

Publisher: Moray Watson

The publisher and authors have done their best to ensure the accuracy and currency of information in Best XI Liverpool; however the publisher accepts no responsibility for the information published herein.

Dedicated to Josefina McLoughlin

About The Authors

Chris Bascombe
Chris is currently the Merseyside Football Reporter for The Daily Telegraph and has been reporting on Liverpool FC since 1998. A former Liverpool FC correspondent for the Liverpool Echo, Chris was named North West Sports Reporter of the Year on five consecutive occasions between 2003-2007. In 2008, he was the ghostwriter of Jamie Carragher's acclaimed autobiography.

Nick Judd
Nick is a football editor and writer who contributes for publications including *FourFourTwo*, *The Independent* and *Champions*. He grew up marvelling at the Liverpool teams of the 1980s and edited the 2012 FA Cup semi-final and final matchday programmes that featured Liverpool.

Ben Lyttleton
Ben is a freelance football journalist and editor who has been writing about Liverpool FC for over 15 years. As the 'neutral' on the *Best XI* selection committee, it was his job to ensure that every player was given a fair chance to make the eleven, and that none of the co-writers came to blows during the decision-making process. This is his third book.

Leo Moynihan
Leo is a freelance sports writer who has written extensively on Liverpool FC for *FourFourTwo* and the *Liverpool Echo*, among others. Ian Rush, John

Barnes, Jamie Carragher, Steven Gerrard and Gerard Houllier are among the prominent figures at Anfield he has interviewed, while he has written a number of books on the club including, *Liverpool: Match of my Life* (re-published by Pitch this year), *The Liverpool Miscellany* and *The Pocket Book of Liverpool*.

Paul Tomkins

A season-ticket holder at Anfield, and author of eight books on Liverpool FC, including *Dynasty: 50 Years of Shankly's Liverpool* and one on Premier League finances, *Pay As You Play*. Paul is a columnist for the official Liverpool website and creator of award-winning site The Tomkins Times.

Paul donated his writer's fee for this book for a good cause - ME research. www.actionforme.org.uk

The Teamsheet

Take two Liverpool fans, put them in a room together, and it's unlikely they would be able to agree on whether Kenny Dalglish's final season as Liverpool coach in 2011-12 was successful, or indeed if King Kenny should have stayed in charge after reaching two Cup finals, and winning one.

Now double that figure, chuck in one neutral to keep the peace, and ask them to name their all-time best eleven team to have played for Liverpool. That's what we did, and while we didn't quite come up with 55 different names, there were some heated debates about certain positions.

The panel certainly knew their stuff: Chris Bascombe is the Merseyside correspondent for *The Daily Telegraph*, Paul Tomkins runs The Tomkins Times, a Liverpool-based website, and has written eight books about the club. Leo Moynihan has written three books about Liverpool, while Nick Judd is an experienced journalist who has been reporting on the Reds for over 15 years.

The spine of this Best XI picked itself: all five of us agreed on Alan Hansen, Steven Gerrard and, yes, Dalglish as the player up front. So far, so easy... But as we turned our attentions to the defence, suddenly the bonhomie evaporated and the Liverpool love gave way to passionate arguments over players and positions.

The goalkeeping decision came down to a straight call between Elisha Scott, the Ireland international who helped Liverpool win two titles in the 1920s and Ray Clemence, a dominant figure throughout Liverpool's successful period in the 1970s. Bruce Grobbelaar and Pepe Reina got passing mentions, but Clemence got the vote, and few would disagree.

The rest of the defence was not so easy, even if Phil Neal was the overwhelming choice at right-back. There were shouts for Rob Jones and Stevie Nicol – one panellist even wanted him at left-back on the back of his outstanding season there in 1987-88, when he was part of a formidable partnership alongside John Barnes (he even scored a hat-trick from there against Newcastle) – but Neal's amazing run of trophies, his consistency and eye for goal in big games, was enough to get the nod.

Hansen's partner at centre-back was the most contentious call in the team: in the first round of votes, there was a five-way tie between Sami Hyppia, Mark Lawrenson, Emlyn Hughes, Phil Thompson and Ron Yeats. Once we realised that left-back was also an issue – with Alec Lindsay and Alan Kennedy in the mix – it allowed us to move Hughes to left-back, where he had played, and reduced the choice in the middle. It finally came down to two men: Lawrenson and Yeats, the Shankly signing who was there as the club began its period of dominance. In the end, sentimentality lost out and it was Lawrenson, now working as a light entertainer... sorry, a co-commentator for the BBC, who completed the defence.

Central midfield was another interesting

battleground, though Gerrard's partner was rarely in doubt. Jimmy Case and Jan Molby were given consideration but Graeme Souness was the overwhelming pick.

Liverpool has a rich history of wide players and it was tough to ignore the claims of the likes of Peter Thompson, Ray Kennedy and Steves Heighway and McManaman. But in the end it came down to pick of two from Billy Liddell, John Barnes and Ian Callaghan. All had compelling cases – Liddell played 534 games in a 23-year career, Barnes lit up Anfield with his wizardry in the late-1980s and early-1990s, while Callaghan, a member of England's 1966 Word Cup squad, made a record 857 appearances for the club. In the end, it was Callaghan who missed the cut.

That just left us with one more position to fill, that of Dalglish's partner up front. Kevin Keegan and Robbie Fowler were in the conversation but it was another unanimous choice: Ian Rush, who topped 30 goals in five of his six full seasons at Liverpool.

The Liverpool Best XI is:

Ray Clemence

Phil Neal

Alan Hansen

Mark Lawrenson

Emlyn Hughes

Billy Liddell

Steven Gerrard

Graeme Souness

John Barnes

Kenny Dalglish

Ian Rush

The formation is 4-4-2, with the emphasis on Graeme Souness holding the midfield together, and Neal and Liddell causing havoc attacking down the right flank. You can just imagine Steven Gerrard combining perfectly with Dalglish, his former boss at the club, through the middle, and the defence is solid given that four of the back five played together in winning the 1978 European Cup final.

1 RAY CLEMENCE

GOALKEEPER

BY LEO MOYNIHAN

Honours First Division Championship 1973 1973, 1976, 1977, 1979, 1980; FA Cup 1974; League Cup 1981; European Cup 1977, 1978, 1981; UEFA Cup 1973, 1976: European Super Cup 1977; Charity Shield - 1974, 1976, 1977, 1979, 1980

In the team because when it came to making saves that not only won football matches, but trophies, Clemence was the greatest

Quote "Ray was one of the best goalkeepers I have ever seen. No-one dominated the box as well as Clem. He made things look easy, was really enthusiastic in training and always wanted people to take shots at him. He defied you to try and put the ball in the net. That's the sign of someone who was always on top of the job and confident in his own ability" – Ian Callaghan

Greatest moment His fine save against Borussia Moenchengladbach with the score at 1-1 in the 1977 European Cup Final

IT WAS A routine that Ray Clemence knew well. Leave the dressing-room for a second half at Anfield, get the gloves on, glance up at the 'This is Anfield' sign, trot down the stairs into the light, up the stairs and turn right for the Kop End.

This time, though, it's different. The dressing-room he has left houses the visiting team, the temptation to touch the sign must be resisted, and as he trots towards the famous Spion Kop, this time he is the man trying to stop those fans' dreams, not help realise them.

This is Clemence's first visit back to the club he served for 14 seasons, playing 665 times, and helping to win 12 major trophies. Liverpool need to win to take the title but are a goal down to Tottenham, the club Clemence chose to join the summer before, despite just winning a third European Cup.

Not many players choose to leave Liverpool. What will the fans' reaction be? As their old goalkeeper gets closer, a ripple of applause behind the goal builds and builds into a tsunami of appreciation and love. Clemence applauds back. Mutual adulation is the order of the day.

"That was the best reception I could ever, ever have considering I made the decision to leave," recalled Clemence. "There were a lot of Liverpool supporters disappointed that I had made it and because of that I wasn't sure of the reception I was going to get when I came back.

"The first half I was playing at the Anfield Road End and they were still chanting, 'England's number one' to me, so that was nice. I could never have envisaged the reception I would get when I came out at half-time and ran down to the Kop.

"The whole stadium stood up, including everyone in the Kop. It was a standing ovation chanting my name. It's probably the most emotional I have ever been at a football ground. It definitely brought a lump to my throat, because I could not believe the reception from them. It was just one of the best moments you could possibly have."

It wasn't a surprise though. The relationship between Liverpool fans, especially those who congregate at the Kop End, and their goalkeepers has long been a special one.

Sam Hardy, the pig-breeder who kept goal for Liverpool when they won the title in 1905-06, the great Irishman Elisha Scott who played 468 games between 1913 and 1934 and, of course, Tommy 'The Flying Pig' Lawrence, who preceded Clemence, all enjoyed a marvellous rapport with the Kop. These days, Pepe Reina speaks with tremendous affection of those who literally have his back and that love goes back for decades.

All were loved, as was Clemence, a man whose prowess for goal prevention brought those same fans honour after honour under both Bill Shankly, and then Bob Paisley.

It was Shankly who, in 1968 paid Scunthorpe

£18,000 for the 18 year-old keeper. Using his penchant for the managerial dark arts, he told the sought-after teenager that his present number one was past it, and that he would be in the first team within six months. It took two and a half years.

"When I got to Liverpool for pre-season after signing for them I found out that Tommy [Lawrence] wasn't over the hill and past his best at all," laughed Clemence. "He was at the peak of his career and I had to wait."

Clemence wasn't alone. Waiting was what new players did at Liverpool. Wait and learn. It was no coincidence that Liverpool's reserve team (according to Shankly, the second best side on Merseyside!) won their league 10 times in 12 years and Clemence, in being part of two of those sides, was educated in what it took to succeed. "It helped the players get into the habit of winning, which is the best habit to have," said Shankly.

Clemence made his debut for the first team in the League Cup against Swansea in September 1968. His next two appearances came a year later in the old European Fairs Cup against Dundalk over two legs. The scores were 10-0 and 4-0 and though you could say that summed up Clemence's career behind an all-conquering Liverpool side, it would be unfair.

Like all great keepers who play in great sides, often they are seen as merely a spectator and it is true there were games when you could have added Clemence to the attendance figures. But his gift lay in his mesmeric levels of concentration and his ability to pull off a superb and vital save at the end of games, the ones that prevented victories from becoming draws and draws becoming defeats.

The Skegness-born keeper was also a big-game player, pulling off penalty saves at vital moments while his two saves in the 1977 European Cup final in Rome – especially his vital block to deny Borussia Moenchengladbach's Uli Stielike – put to bed any notion of him being simply a decent keeper in a fantastic team.

Clemence got his chance as Liverpool's regular number one in 1970 after Shankly's side crashed out of the FA Cup, going down 1-0 to second division Watford. On the way home from Hertfordshire, the great manager realised he had to change the team. It was hard but the players who had made Liverpool great were past their sell-by date and youth had to be given its chance. The following game, Clemence was in (he'd only miss six league games in the next 11 years) and a new, brilliant side began to take shape.

The 1971 FA Cup final was lost to Arsenal and they were pipped to the 1972 league title by Derby but there were signs of greatness, stemming from the keeper who was quickly seen as one of the best around. Clemence made his international debut (the first of 56 he won whilst a Liverpool player, a number dramatically affected by his sharing the gloves with Peter Shilton) in November 1972 and later that season had the first of his five league titles and a UEFA Cup winner's medal, as Liverpool made their first victorious move on the continent.

It was in the first leg of the final – Moenchengladbach were the opponents – that Clemence proved he was every bit the match-winner. Liverpool had stormed to a 3-0 win but the Germans kept pushing for an away goal and were awarded a penalty at the Kop End.

German international Jupp Heynckes stepped up and hit a fine spot-kick, low to Clemence's right, but in a flash of green and red, the ball was turned wide for a corner. "What a save!" recalled Tommy Smith. "The Kop went nuts. That was the loudest cheer of the night." The Germans went on to win 2-0 in the second leg, underlining just how vital Clemence's contribution had been.

In 1976, again in the UEFA Cup, Clemence made another remarkable penalty save, this time to deny Dynamo Dresden's Peter Kotte and secure a 0-0 draw on the way to another winner's medal (apparently Paisley had seen Kotte take one the week before and told Clemence which way to go).

Athletic, enthusiastic, switched on and a great organiser, Clemence was the eyes behind the team. "I owed a great deal to Ray, a great communicator who would virtually talk me through games," said Alan Hansen. "Ray was brilliant, repeatedly shouting instructions about my positioning."

With Liverpool dominating games and often holding a high line, he was also a very modern keeper, able to sweep behind his defenders, whilst at crosses he would dominate, often starting another attack with his quick and accurate distribution.

Shankly's last game in charge was the 3-0 FA Cup Final win over Newcastle, and the manager who signed Clemence was in no doubt of the talent he had unearthed. "We had a great team in the Sixties. But if we'd had Ray Clemence in goal then we'd have won the European Cup and all the cups under the sun.

"I say that because I think Ray Clemence was one of the greatest goalkeepers of all time. If he'd have been in that 1960s team, I don't think anybody could possibly have beaten us."

Under Bob Paisley, the team and its keeper got even better, making a successful charge for the European Cup in 1977. Clemence played his part. An athletic save thwarted Saint-Etienne at Anfield in the iconic quarter-final, allowing David Fairclough to snatch a famous win and in the final that save at 1-1 from Stielike was a again the springboard to the glory that followed.

"When people ask me what was my best save, I tend to rate them for their importance, for what they meant," said Clemence. "In Rome, Stielike broke through onto to a ball over the top. It was one against one, a situation I'd been brought up and trained to deal with at Liverpool, and I blocked his shot with my knees. No save has been more critical than that one."

Two minutes later Liverpool were 2-1 up and the trophy was coming to Merseyside for the first of its five visits. "It was the turning point of the game," said Paisley. "Ray might have made more spectacular saves but I doubt he has made a more important one. The Germans never recovered from it."

The European champions defended their title the following season and the 1978-79 season saw the side – now boasting the talents of Kenny Dalglish, Graeme Souness and Alan Hansen - steamroller the opposition, with Clemence conceding only 16 league goals, a new record.

Things looked easy. Were they? "When you play behind Liverpool's defence over 12 years, I didn't have lots to do," admitted Clemence. "If you had one or two saves to make in the game, it was all about making those saves. That was part of the make-up of the Liverpool goalkeeper."

His last Championship title came in 1980 and another (his third) European Cup a year later after a 1-0 win over Real Madrid in Paris. That night was a turning point. In the Parc des Princes dressing-room amid the pop, pop, pop of champagne bottles, the keeper sat quietly, contemplating his future.

"It was just another day at the office for me," Clemence remembered. "It was there and then that I made the decision that to perform at the level I had always pushed myself to, I just needed a new challenge.

"I had won everything there was to win at Liverpool. I was 32 years of age and for me to play longer at the level I wanted to play I just needed a new challenge."

On 8 June 1981 Clemence knocked on his manager's door and explained his decision: he wanted to leave.

"When he came to me and asked for a transfer, I tried to change his mind," said Paisley. "He was the greatest goalkeeper I've seen. He had the edge on [Peter] Shilton. But in the end we agreed to Ray's request and at a bargain price.

"If it hadn't been for his great service the fee would have been not a penny under £450,000 rather than the £300,000 Keith Burkinshaw paid to take him to Tottenham. That was 'washers' for the best goalkeeper in the country."

2 PHIL NEAL

RIGHT FULL-BACK

BY LEO MOYNIHAN

Honours First Division Championship 1976, 1977, 1979, 1980, 1982, 1983, 1984, 1986; European Cup 1977, 1978, 1980, 1982; UEFA Cup 1976; League Cup 1981, 1982, 1983, 1984, Charity Shield 1976, 1977, 1979, 1980, 1982; European SuperCup 1977

In the team because Neal was the most consistent right-back Liverpool have ever had, winning four European Cups, and scoring in two finals.

Quote "Phil adds an extra dimension to the team with his ability to surge forward and set things up. He's got a tremendous awareness of every other player in the side and what their job is. I suppose he picked it up in his utility days at Northampton – in fact he often tells me he's a better goalkeeper than I am!" – Ray Clemence

Best Moment Stroking the ball past Borussia Moenchengladbach's goalkeeper from the penalty-spot to seal Liverpool's first European Cup triumph in Rome

PICTURE THE SCENE. It's late September 1983, a night match at Anfield. Two Koppites meet in their usual pub, have a few pints of the usual, share the usual debates and laughs, take their usual route to the ground, move toward their usual spot behind the goal, sing the usual songs and await their usual heroes.

Out come the players. All seems normal but then one fan turns to his companion. "Something's not right," he says.

"I know what you mean, but I can't put my finger on it," replies his mate.

"Grobbelaar is there. Hansen, Souness, Kenny."

"Hold on! Where the hell is Phil Neal?"

They were right. For the first time in an incredible 417 matches, there was no Phil Neal. The last game the popular right-back had missed had been in the autumn of 1976. Since then, governments had fallen, Prime Ministers replaced, children had grown up and under Bob Paisley, Liverpool had gone from being one of the best clubs in England to the best in Europe.

The best in Europe. On three occasions, Neal and Liverpool had been crowned European champions and by the end of that same season, they did it again. Once more, it was in Rome. This time, Neal was the sole survivor from the 1977 team that had left the Eternal City victorious.

Neal played more than his part, not only

shackling the attacking instincts of Europe's finest forwards but scoring in both Rome finals, highlighting just how vital he was going forward as well as defensively.

In short, Neal was Liverpool's 'Mr. Consistent', giving so much to the team and to the fans who followed it. His presence was never taken for granted but Neal himself knew the importance of not missing games, especially at a club where being injured often meant being forgotten.

"There were two occasions when I could have missed a game," he said of his 417-game run in the side. "One was when I got a fractured cheekbone. Roger Davis, the centre-forward at Derby, gave me an elbow [in January 1976]. I went in on the Sunday and had my cheekbone lifted in line with the rest of my face to put my face back in shape.

"Come the middle of the week, I was walking around the training ground watching the players train. We were playing West Ham that Saturday. Bob Paisley came to me on Wednesday and said, 'How you feeling?'. I said, 'I' okay. I'm over the op and everything else.' I chose to play, against the specialist's wishes, as he said that I shouldn't play for a month. I got away with it."

Quite rightly, much is made of Paisley's fantastic record in the transfer market and there is no better indication of that brilliance than with Neal, his first signing in October 1974. Paisley had sent his trusted scout Geoff Twentyman to watch Neal, who had been playing for Northampton since he was 16. He'd heard good things but now it was time to have a look with his own beady eyes.

Neal only played the first 20 minutes at right-back, before replacing injured goalkeeper Alan Starling between the sticks. Paisley had seen enough and soon a cheque for £66,000 was making its way to the Cobblers. The Liverpool coach had his first new recruit.

Neal arrived from the Fourth Division as a possible replacement for an ageing Alec Lindsey at left-back or as cover for Chris Lawler, himself a fine goalscoring right-back and wonderful servant to the club. He might have expected a long spell in the reserves but he got his chance much sooner than he thought.

Neal had played just four games of second-string football before getting an unexpected nod in the biggest of matches. "It was a Saturday morning and I was all prepared to play for the reserves, whilst the first team had a derby at Goodison," recalled Neal. "Tom Saunders, Bob's advisor, came round to my digs that morning and said there was a problem with one of the full-backs and so Bob wanted me to join them.

"I was a little nervous, but I thought, 'Part of the squad, okay, that's fine'. We went to Anfield to pick up my boots and I asked if we would be taking the car and Tom is like, 'No, we'll walk across the park'. So there I am walking to Goodison with my boots in a brown paper bag and thousands of Scousers all asking me for tickets. This is my first experience of the Merseyside derby, remember, and I couldn't believe how electric the atmosphere was.

"I was just enjoying taking in the whole day, enjoying the occasion, but then I walk into the dressing-room. 'Get ready son,' says Bob. 'You're playing.' I never had the chance to phone my Mum or anything. I went out in front of the crowd and I thought, 'If I can cope with this then I can cope with anything that life throws at me,' and I did. That day was my base.

"We drew 0-0 and I jumped for joy, cuddling Emlyn Hughes like we'd won the League. There's 56,000 fans thinking, 'Who the heck is this fella?'."

Liverpool finished that season second in the league, and without a trophy. Like the goalless draw at Goodison, Neal wrongly thought this was a decent result but with the team being moulded to suit the new manager, he would soon realise that second best would just not do.

Neal had played the last half of the season at left-back but would now be the regular right-back and once there, there would be no budging him for a full decade. "Phil was 'Mr. Dependable'," said Alan Hansen, another integral part of Liverpool's stingy defence. "A player with wonderful positional sense who went about his job in the steadiest, most disciplined way."

Dependable, disciplined, steady. You could

argue that these attributes are a little unfair on Neal. Lee Dixon or Nigel Winterburn are steady and dependable full-backs. Neal from right-back offered a dynamism so often lacking in full-backs unwilling to go over the half-way line. Neal wasn't that type.

His footballing brain meant wingers rarely got a look-in but his attacking enthusiasm was never dulled by his manager. By overloading the right-wing, opponents had one more player to worry about, and his teammates one more option to consider. No wonder the Kop nicknamed him 'Zico'.

Neal won his first trophies in 1976, helping Paisley win the League and the Uefa Cup. The following season, the title was won again, the FA Cup Final lost and so then to Rome for the European Cup showpiece. Neal had enjoyed a fine game and with eight minutes to go and his side 2-1 up he had the responsibility of stepping up to take a penalty that would seal the deal.

"The ref pointed to the spot and my first reaction is, 'Oh Christ, it's all on me now!'" remembered Neal. "I'm 50 yards away and I have to make what felt like a hell of a long walk to the penalty box. Emlyn [Hughes] looks at me with desperation in his eyes, Smithy [Tommy Smith] looks at me with one of those, 'Score this or I'm breaking your fucking back' stares and Cally [Ian Callaghan] who had never been booked and is so quiet and polite shouts, 'Hey, Nealy, stick this in will ya'."

As ever, he did stick it in and it was time to party. The celebrations went on into the morning, and by the pool it was obvious some people were going to have to go in.

"I had brought some new shoes from Russell and Bromley (English, elegant and dependable, just like Neal!) for about £80 which was quite a few quid back in 1977, and Kevin [Keegan] is trying to get me in. 'I've got a shitty watch on that I don't care about, but let me get my Russell and Bromleys off!' I cried.

"Kevin was having none of it and in the play-struggle I caught him under the eye with my thumb. Kevin came home with a real shiner and the press were adamant that Smithy had hit him, but it wasn't that at all. It was me trying to protect my new shoes."

Neal had won the first of his 50 England caps in 1976 and it was the season of his last run out for his country that he was once again crowned a European champion. That 1983-84 campaign saw Liverpool take three trophies – the League, the League Cup and the European Cup, with Neal once again scoring in Rome to help his team to a famous victory.

With Graeme Souness departing after that final, Joe Fagan turned to Neal to be his skipper and whilst the team suffered from a term of transition, they again reached the European Cup Final. This time, it was in the Heysel Stadium in Brussels.

Neal went to Belgium knowing that if he was to win a fifth winner's medal he would be joining an exclusive club occupied only by three Real Madrid mainstays; Alfredo Di Stefano, Francisco Gento (who won six) and Marquitos. It was heady company befitting such a stylish performer but personal accolades were soon forgotten on a night full only of tragedy and shame.

A new era dawned at Anfield post-Heysel and whilst Neal's name was strongly touted as Fagan's successor as manager at Anfield, the board instead chose Kenny Dalglish. Neal lost the captaincy to Alan Hansen and soon lost his place to the young and equally as consistent Steve Nicol.

Nicol, like Lawler in the 1960s and 1970s, and going back further to Bill Dunlop in the early-1900s, was a typically dependable Liverpool right-back. So amongst such exulted company why should Neal be afforded the honour of making this best eleven? It's hard to better his tactically astute game which helped both defence and attack. He was a mix of solidity and craft, two-footed, a good tackler and cool under pressure.

"Neal was like a top golfer, according to Geoff Twentyman: he was able to chip, drive and weight the ball perfectly, and on both flanks," wrote John Williams in *Red Men: Liverpool Football Club*, a fantastic biography of the club. "He was simply the most consistent and most reliable outfield player in Liverpool's history. Neal is the only Liverpool player to win four European Cups, and he played in five finals, while also winning eight league championships. He became the ever-present defensive rock of the Bob Paisley era, a wonderful servant, without doubt one of the club's greatest ever players."

In November 1985, Neal played the last of his 650 games for Liverpool (if you count his games for Northampton, Bolton and England, he played almost 1,000 times), ending his career with 59 goals to his name.

Time moved on, even for Neal but no doubt, those two Koppites in their usual spot behind the goal will, even today, concede that it's not the same without him.

3 ALAN HANSEN

CENTRE BACK

BY NICK JUDD

Honours First Division Championship 1979, 1980, 1982, 1983, 1984, 1986, 1988, 1990; European Cups 1978, 1981, 1984; FA Cup 1986, 1989 League Cups 1981, 1983, 1984; Charity Shield 1979, 1980, 1981, 1983, 1987, 1990)

In the side because... he was composed, a superb reader of the game who led the side with distinction

Quote "Quite simply the most skilful centre-half I've ever seen in British football. He has such beautiful balance. When he carries the ball he never loses control and always looks so graceful. He's a joy to watch" – Bob Paisley

Greatest moment Winning the Double as captain in 1986, as Liverpool became only the third side of the 20th century to lift both the league and FA Cup in one season

SATURDAY MAY 10, 1986; the weather is sultry, the atmosphere charged. The stadium represents a city divided by red and blue.

At 3.45pm the Liverpool players make the long walk back to their Wembley dressing-room, the furthest of the two, and sit dejected, exhausted.

They are losing to fierce rivals Everton in the FA Cup final, a competition that has eluded them since 1974. The street parties that preceded the game are over. The Reds are desperate to make history, the Blues to stop it. It all boils down to the next 45 minutes.

Alan Hansen, who believed the club was jinxed in the FA Cup, had experienced a mixed week: he had celebrated winning the league title as captain seven days earlier in an unusually uninhibited manner at Stamford Bridge, before being left out of Scotland's squad for the 1986 World Cup in Mexico.

At Wembley, though, Hansen had been at fault for Gary Lineker's opening goal in the first half, but there is no blame from his teammates, no accusations. Win as a team, lose as a team. Hansen has led by example all season, hardly putting a foot wrong.

Dalglish then delivers a rousing team-talk – "I don't want any regrets. This is it. Let's have a right go" – and it inspires Hansen's teammates in the shadows of the Twin Towers. Two goals from Ian Rush, a third from Craig Johnston and a barnstorming performance from midfielder Kevin MacDonald and the jinx comes to an end. Liverpool win their first Double, and it comes at Everton's expense.

Even the experienced members of the squad, players who had lifted league titles, League Cups and conquered Europe, are ecstatic. The sea of red in the Wembley stands, like their heroes so used to success already, sways with pride.

As Hansen followed his manager up the 39 steps en route to becoming only the third captain to have lifted the League and FA Cup title in one season, he pauses. Dalglish stops.

"Just getting my breath back, gaffer," Hansen explains, before sprinting ahead of his manager in an effort to get to the trophy first. "The cheek!" laughed Dalglish in his autobiography. "He deserved it though. Al had contributed another superb season for grateful employers."

The moment Hansen lifted that FA Cup above his head was the pinnacle of, at that time, nine glorious years at a club that 15 years earlier had stated that the same player "did not reach the standard required" following a four-day trial. Suffice to say that Hansen's first correspondence from Liverpool Football Club gave no indication of the glittering career that would follow, or cause Dalglish to hail him as "one of the greatest central defenders of his time".

The Scot won 17 titles, the same number as his golfing hero Jack Nicklaus. As well as winning six league titles, he became the first player to win the league championship in three separate decades. He won three European Cup winners' medals, two FA Cups, three League Cups and six Charity Shields. Consistent, composed and calculated, he was the cornerstone of four Liverpool sides.

Hansen was born in the mining town of Sauchie – "You either played football or played football," he recalled – but Hansen started life as a promising golfer. "That's what I wanted to be." He even represented his country at the sport – as well as volleyball and squash – and boasted a handicap of two by the age of 16, but quickly realised swinging clubs wouldn't pay the bills.

Instead he combined an office job at a motor insurance company (after he had been rejected to become a PE teacher) with a part-time playing contract at Partick Thistle, where his brother John was on the books. He brought in a combined wage of £40 a week.

Hansen made more than 100 appearances for Thistle and helped them win promotion to the Scottish Premier League in 1976. He was lean in stature but big in presence, imperious even, initially as an attacking midfielder but mainly in defence. His performances earned call ups to Scotland's Under-21 and Under-23 sides.

"That was when we reappeared on the scene," recalled Liverpool's Youth Development Officer Tom Saunders. "We had been keeping an eye on him for the best part of two years. He was a good reader of the game, possessed good control and passed the ball well."

Liverpool scout Geoff Twentyman, who had sent that rejection letter six years earlier, agreed, suggesting Hansen "made everything look so easy". In 1977, weeks after Liverpool's league and European Cup Double, the excited but "frightened"

21-year-old signed for £100,000.

Hansen was touted by *Shoot!* magazine as one of "soccer's most talented young men" who, it claimed, wouldn't let Liverpool down. They were right, of course, but he had to wait before becoming a first-team regular.

He was given his first opportunity after established centre-back Emlyn Hughes was injured, making his debut aged 22 in September 1977 against Derby County. He was voted Man of the Match by one journalist, Don Jones, who awarded him nine out of ten and described him as the "new Spion Kop hero". Ray Clemence was also impressed, suggesting the new Scot "could add six years to my career".

However, with Hansen still developing and Liverpool boasting a settled and successful back four, he had to settle for sporadic opportunities, which brought a degree of inconsistency. His forward forays, which later became one of his trademarks, led manager Paisley to warn: "Just watch it, will you? I'm still too young to have a heart attack." Hansen himself admitted he found it hard being in and out of the team.

He won a regular place in the side towards the end of his first season, at left-back, a campaign which culminated in the 1977 European Cup Final against Bruges. Hansen's best was yet to come, of course, but winning an early medal took some of the pressure off.

Still, he was his own biggest critic. "I couldn't tackle," Hansen explained modestly in his autobiography. "I was no more than average in the air and my level of determination and aggression left a lot to be desired. My pace and technical ability were not always enough to enable me to do my job properly." What he failed to mention was that he had two good feet, he read the game with aplomb and he loved to get forward.

It was Hansen's industry at Melwood that helped him establish his place in the 1978-79 team, considered by many the best Liverpool team ever, moving to the centre from left-back after Hughes moved to Wolves. At the end of the campaign, the side won the league after conceding just 16 goals. "That will never be beaten," he said.

With regular games – he made his 50th appearance less than two years after joining he club – came increasing confidence and maturity. Hansen had admitted he was homesick in the early stages of his move but things changed when he committed to the club, and the area, by buying a property of his own in Southport.

Off the field, Hansen was a popular figure with good habits. "He was elegance on long legs, and bright with it," recalled Dalglish. "Meticulously neat and tidy," remembered Ian Rush.

He was a stable part of the dressing-room, although he suffered from terrible nerves before games which he put down to the unique and relentless pressure to win matches that came with playing for Liverpool in that era.

"Al would be absolutely silent, legs crossed, reading the programme, lost in reflection," recalled Dalglish of Hansen's pre-match nerves. "I spent most of the time going to and from the toilet," Hansen admitted.

On the pitch, Hansen shed his inhibitions. As well as tremendous pace over long distances and an unrivalled awareness, he exhibited class with the ball at his feet, more often than not trying to find the feet of the flair players.

Few strikers got the better of him around his own area. Hansen was belligerent, keen to stay on his feet. He was never sent off, yellow cards were a rarity and together with Phil Thompson, and later Mark Lawrenson, he forged a telepathic understanding with those around him. "Strengths and weaknesses," he said. "We played to our strengths and exploited their weaknesses."

As Hansen grew more accustomed to the rigours of success, so his presence in the dressing-room grew as he developed a more professional, and winning, attitude. He ingratiated himself in the club's hunger for triumph. He won two European Cups in the 1980s and four League Cups in a row. He made 50 or more appearances in eight consecutive seasons.

This growing sense of responsibility culminated in Hansen getting the captain's armband from his close friend Dalglish, who was Liverpool boss by then, before a pre-season match against Brighton. The honour came as a surprise to him.

"In terms of my idea of what a captain should be like, I was never one," he explained. His manager disagreed. Dalglish not only thought Hansen had the necessary leadership qualities, he also believed Hansen was a lucky charm.

"Al deserved to be captain," said Dalglish. "He held the respect of the dressing room, and everybody wanted to be friends with him. He was incredibly popular. He presented many credentials for captaincy. What set Al apart was that Lady Luck had a serious crush on Liverpool's number six. Never in my life have I encountered somebody so frequently blessed with good fortune as Alan Hansen."

Hansen may have overseen two Doubles – first in 1986 and again in 1989 – but ironically, it was bad luck with persistent knee injuries that brought Hansen's career to an end during the 1990-91 season, little more than a year after making his 600th appearance. He encountered more highs than lows, but the psychological effect of staying at the top for so long, not to mention the tragedies of Heysel and Hillsborough, had a profound effect.

He retired, a club legend, shortly after Dalglish's resignation in March 1991. Hansen was tipped to take over the club's reserves and one day manage the club, but he instead opted for a career in broadcasting.

4 MARK LAWRENSON

CENTRE BACK

BY LEO MOYNIHAN

Honours First Division Championship 1982, 1983, 1984, 1986, 1988; FA Cup 1986; European Cup 1984; League Cup 1982, 1983, 1984; Charity Shield 1982, 1986

In the team because there have been plenty of great individual centre backs at Liverpool, but never as good a combination of Lawrenson and Hansen

Quote "No matter how much he grates you on the TV with some of the things he comes out with and the voice on him, you can't deny his genius on the football field" – Dave Kirby, Liverpudlian playwright

Greatest Moment His towering header against Tottenham at the Kop End that helped Liverpool take the 1981-82 title

MARK LAWRENSON HAD options. Lots of them. His four years at Brighton had cemented his reputation in the English game and plenty of managers were interested in signing a player comfortable across the back four and the midfield.

Most eager was Ron Atkinson. Recently appointed at Manchester United, the Old Trafford manager was full of big plans for the biggest club with the biggest ground. The new man had ideas and was building a new team that would soon include English sensation Bryan Robson, bought for a British record transfer fee of £1.5m.

Then along came scruffy Bob Paisley, wearing his old cardigan and his old slippers. Atkinson, all bling and cigars, believed he had got his man but a late meeting with Liverpool changed everything. The contracts were signed before Paisley arranged to meet Lawrenson the following day at a hotel to take him for his medical.

"I was as nervous as a kitten, with my best suit, shirt, tie on, best bib and tucker," recalled the Preston-born Lawrenson. "I went down to reception and the doorman told me, 'Mr Paisley is waiting for you in his car outside.'

"When I got to the car I saw that Bob was wearing slippers and a cardigan. I was waiting for Jeremy Beadle to pop up. I couldn't believe it. That was my first encounter with Bob Paisley and I knew I'd come to the right place. They'd just won the European Cup and there was this fellow, who everyone in football thought was this absolute god, driving me around in his slippers and cardigan. 'You'll do for me!'"

Liverpool may have won a third European Cup

just months before, but they had finished fifth in the First Division, a position deemed as failure for a club like Liverpool, now so accustomed to topping the pile.

Paisley – not one to sit polishing his trophies, not even a (still) unprecedented third European Cup – set about bringing in new faces. Ronnie Whelan, Bruce Grobbelaar, Craig Johnston and Ian Rush would all break into the first team that season and in Lawrenson, Paisley was attracted to his all-round skill rather than his obvious versatility.

"Sometimes the problem with players who can fill a number of roles is that while they're useful jacks of all trades, they're masters of none," commented Paisley later. "But wherever Mark plays, he does it brilliantly. He was my three-in-one signing because he can go in at centre-back, left-back or midfield and perform with equal quality."

The £900,00 fee was a club record (Liverpool had actually turned down the chance to sign him in 1977 as they weren't prepared to pay £100,000) but here was a player that managers might love, but teammates less so. At first it seemed that centre-back Phil Thompson should be wary of the new man, but then maybe Ray Kennedy at left-midfield, or even Terry McDermott in the centre. The first man to lose his spot, though, was Alan Kennedy, as Lawrenson started at left-back.

It was a debut at Wolves that he had to wait

for. "When I first spoke to the club I didn't tell them I had been sent off pre-season playing for Brighton and that I was going to be suspended for a few games," said Lawrenson. "I thought if I said anything about it they wouldn't take me. You are so keen to come to a club like Liverpool that you don't want to jeopardise it. Looking back it's silly, because maybe Bob would have liked the fact that I had a bit of the devil in me."

Liverpool needed some of that devil to turn around a terrible start to the season that saw them languishing, after a 3-1 home defeat to Manchester City on Boxing Day, in 12th place.

As a new team, Liverpool were struggling but Lawrenson was impressing with his ability in the number of positions he was asked to fill. Composed, strong and elegant, Lawrenson looked very much at home at Anfield but quickly got a taste of just how meticulous his manager was.

"I remember a game at Arsenal that we won comfortably and which was the game on *Match of the Day*. I did a little trick, a neat little step-over to sell a dummy to one of the Arsenal strikers and it had been highlighted by Jimmy Hill. When I walked into the training on the Monday, Bob came over. 'Did you watch *Match of the Day?*' he asked. 'Yes.' 'Well, just remember that millions of others did too and every bloody forward in the country will be aware of that little trick now.' Then he explained: 'Playing for Liverpool, everything is highlighted and people are always watching you'."

Soon, those teams going for the title were

watching Liverpool too, and with the new players excelling during a 14-game unbeaten run, they needed a win against Tottenham at Anfield in the season's penultimate fixture to seal an unlikely title.

An incredible Glenn Hoddle goal in the first half gave the visitors a half-time advantage but attacking the Kop End, Liverpool raised the ante and just six minutes into the second period, Lawrenson towered above the Spurs' defence to power a header into the top corner past the despairing Ray Clemence. Kenny Dalglish (thanks to a Lawrenson assist) and Ronnie Whelan settled matters and the title was back in L4.

It was huge moment for Lawrenson and one that endeared him to a delighted Kop. He had started the game in centre-midfield, a position he would start the following campaign, but on 28 December 1982 he was handed the number four shirt from Phil Thompson and played alongside Alan Hansen. This time the partnership was for keeps and to many it is among the best central defensive relationships ever seen – not only at Liverpool, but in the history of the British game.

In a way, Lawrenson's versatility made him the ideal Liverpool centre-back. Yes, he could head the ball and yes, he was an exceptional tackler but having played at full-back and in midfield, he proved he could carry the ball, play a bit, pass and move. Alongside the stylish Hansen, it was perfect.

Lawrenson was faster than the ousted

Thompson (himself a fine centre-half) but also possessed his predecessor's erudite skills. "Fortunately we had cerebral defenders in Alan Hansen and Lawro," said Ian Rush. "Rather than winning the ball through crunching tackles, they possessed such vision and reading of a game they won much of the ball through interception. Then, rather than humping the ball forward, they had the ability to bring the ball out of defence, allowing us to maintain possession and affect better movement upfront."

Lawrenson scoffs at the idea that he and Hansen were all elegance and flowing football but they were just as effective with and without the ball. "Whenever we got possession we were told to get it forward," he says. "To be fair, with Kenny around there was little else you could do. If he made a run and didn't get it, my God, you got a bollocking. 'Get it out of your feet and get the ball forward!' he would say, but the important thing was accuracy. If you knocked it six inches wrong to Kenny, you got a blast."

It was said that Liverpool's best defender was Ian Rush, such was his work-rate; equally, you could argue that the team's most effective offensive duo were Hansen and Lawrenson, as they started moves with accurate passes to their skilful and demanding front men.

When opponents did get behind the defence

they often found themselves pick-pocketed by a Lawrenson tackle. His telescopic leg would steal the glory they were sure was about to be theirs.

"He's probably the best tackler in the box I've ever seen," enthused Paisley. "A mistimed challenge in the penalty area can be costly but Mark nicks the ball off people as clean as a whistle. Like a thief in the night, he's in and got the ball before his opponent even realises it."

The title was regained in 1982-83 with plenty to spare before coming back to the Anfield trophy cabinet the following season for a third year in a row. "Do you know, I never even realised we'd done that," says Lawrenson. "It sounds terribly blasé, doesn't it? That's just how the club wanted it though. Any success was played down and you learnt not to dwell on what you'd achieved, but to just get on with winning more.

"We'd get our championship winners medals on the first day of pre-season. Ronnie Moran would walk in with a shoe-box full of them and ask us: 'Did you play 14 league games last season? Yes? Here you go. Twelve? Oh, unlucky.' It was so matter of fact."

For those two seasons, Lawrenson was playing in what was seen all over Europe as the best central defensive partnership there was and despite the nonchalant manner in which they viewed success, there was no let up in actually achieving it.

Such was his form, Lawrenson even managed to convince legends of the game (and his club) to call it a day. In January 1984, Newcastle came to Anfield in the FA Cup. The Magpies were flying high in the old Second Division and in Kevin Keegan they had a talisman who would propel them back to the top-flight.

Liverpool swept them to one side that night, winning 4-0 and there was an incident in the game that made Keegan think about his own footballing mortality. With a ball played into the channel, Keegan had a four-yard start on Lawrenson. It was an opening that the eager striker would have hoped to snatch but with three huge bounds, the Liverpool defender was past him, had won the ball and was away.

Keegan felt he had had the rug pulled out from under his feet. In his mind, he was too slow and a few weeks later announced he would call it a day at the end of the season. In retrospect, the player the Kop once called 'Mighty Mouse' might have been harsh on himself. Lawrenson after all, could and would make the most spritely of young strikers look slow, such was his turn of pace and timing of a tackle.

1983-84 saw the League Cup won for a fourth year in a row, whilst another foraging run to a European Cup final brought further glory. Liverpool played 67 games that season, and Lawrenson missed only one, the League Cup semi-final first leg at Walsall.

There was no fatigue but there was the odd

blip. A 4-0 defeat at Coventry that season was a case of a *very* bad day at the office and for the two stalwarts at the back to let such a thing happen was, well, strange. "Tell me that won't happen again?" asked Joe Fagan on the Monday morning. "No gaffer, it won't happen again." "Good, let's go training."

The European Cup Final in Rome against Roma underlined the class and temperament of Lawrenson who, despite the surroundings and the quality of the opposition, stifled the home team and in doing so nullified and frustrated the locals so that towards the end of the game all you could hear were the dulcet tones of travelling Scousers.

How impressed the Italian purists watching the final must have been. Here was a player who could read a game, read a forward and squeeze the life out of both: *catenaccio* with a Lancashire accent and a moustache.

Lawrenson remained at Hansen's side the following season. It was to be Joe Fagan's last and would end in tragedy at Heysel. Lawrenson dislocated his shoulder in the final that night after only three minutes. It mattered little of course.

Kenny Dalglish took the reins just days later and Lawrenson was a valued member of his Double-winning squad the following season. The emergence of Gary Gillespie brought competition for places but with Bob Paisley advising the new player-manager, Lawrenson's versatility was not forgotten and often he would slip into his midfield role, chipping in with the odd goal including a vital one at Chelsea in the fourth round of the FA Cup.

Stamford Bridge was the venue for the last game of the season and once again Lawrenson, wearing the number 10 shirt, played in midfield for the ill Jan Molby. A bug took Gillespie out that week too, and with Molby fit again, Dalglish was spared a selection problem and so it was Lawrenson and Hansen for the FA Cup final against Everton the following Saturday.

It was a memorable day and Lawrenson, like the team, got to grips with a good Everton side, eventually stubbing out the threat of Gary Lineker and Graeme Sharp. Rush did his thing at the other end and the Double was won.

Lawrenson happily filed the role of utility man the following campaign but a ruptured Achilles tendon in the March of 1987 was to signal the beginning of the end for the leggy defender. He returned and played a part in the 1987-88 season but he admitted that things weren't right and it says much for his ability that he could play without observers knowing there was a problem.

"None of the other Liverpool players in the Liverpool side had any idea how badly I was struggling," Lawrenson remembers. "They were playing so well and winning that their performances masked my weaknesses. When I got back into the team, I found I couldn't turn and run like I used to be able to do.

"I was just getting by on my positional play

and my experience. I found I was a yard slower than everyone else and I couldn't get away with it against top-class teams. When Arsenal's Martin Hayes beat me to the ball over 20 yards twice in a minute, I looked at the bench and knew it was time to pack it in. It came as a complete bombshell to Kenny Dalglish.

"When the surgeon and I told him, he was speechless. I just couldn't run at all. My Achilles is two-and-a-half times bigger in my right leg now. I suppose, from a certain point of view, I did well to hide my injury from everyone. But even though I was playing on with the injury, it was demoralising and frustrating and, for someone who takes pride in his performance, I was terribly disappointed inwardly."

Lawrenson departed after playing 356 times for Liverpool, scoring 18 goals on the way. A brief spell managing and coaching preceded a career in punditry and whilst there are many Koppites who might not enjoy him on their television screens, you won't find one who didn't love him in the red of their football team.

5 EMLYN HUGHES

LEFT FULL-BACK

BY NICK JUDD

Honours First Division Championship 1973, 1976, 1977, 1979; FA Cup 1974; European Cup 1977, 1978; UEFA Cup 1973, 1976; European Super Cup 1977; Charity Shield 1974, 1976, 1977

He's in the side because... he was loyal, captained the side with distinction, and was an integral part of the side that conquered England and Europe in the late 1960s and 1970s

Quote "He was an absolute legend. When I went to Liverpool he was the main man. He was a wonderful player and a fantastic example to everyone. He was the best person to learn from and a larger than life character" – Graeme Souness

Greatest moment Winning the European Cup as captain in 1977. He was the first Liverpool player to lift 'the Cup with the Big Ears'

LIVERPOOL SUPPORTERS HAVE always recognised, acknowledged and celebrated excellence, particularly from those in red. Yet in the 1979-80 season, it was a player wearing gold and black who received as warm a welcome as anyone coming out of the home dressing-room. That's because for the previous 12-and-a-half years, he had done exactly that.

A warm applause gathered momentum. Fans rose to their feet. The claps were accompanied by an appreciative roar of approval until all four stands were united in a heartfelt outpouring of appreciation.

The feeling was reciprocated even if Emlyn Hughes, then in Wolves colours, was tearful. He had loved every second of his Anfield stay before moving to Molineux in 1979. He had played at left-back, centre-back and centre-midfield. Wherever he was asked, it didn't matter.

He had won 13 winners' medals, eleven as captain, including the European Cup. Twice. His arrival had provided the Kop with a new hero. More importantly, he played the game with boundless energy, an unwavering passion and never-say-die attitude that encapsulated the depth of feeling from the supporters. He was a hero and a gallant number six, a loveable lunatic with an infectious smile.

Hughes's formative football steps gave little clue to the astonishing career that lay ahead. He grew up in Barrow and had a rugby-loving dad, Fred, who toured with the British Lions in 1946. Emlyn excelled with balls, both egg-shaped and round, and while his father hoped his son would follow in his footsteps, Hughes junior always preferred football. He was good, too, and he believed in his ability, even at a young age.

"If this boy was as good at football as he thinks

he is, he would play for England," read Hughes's school report. Little did his teacher know how prophetic their words would be, yet Hughes knew that his dream required hard work and sacrifice and he wasn't afraid to consider a plan B. "I know it's important to have some security to fall back on if the gamble in football doesn't come off," he told a young Jimmy Armfield in 1964.

He needn't have worried, although his first club, Blackpool, needed convincing. Hughes was taken on trial thanks largely to his father's persuasive nature, and the fact that he was friends with Tangerines' boss Ron Suart. Hughes was deemed too small and told to come back in 12 months. In that year, Hughes shot up, thanks to what Liverpool boss Bob Paisley later described as a combination of "steaks and youth games".

Hughes also moved to Blackpool to focus on his training and he ended up lodging with future World Cup winner Alan Ball. He worked on his pace - "a full-back must be able to keep up with a fast winger," he said – and studied video footage of players in his position.

In 1964, he was offered a contract at £8 a week, to which he said: "Yes, quicker than a girl does to a marriage proposal." He had to wait until 1965-66 to make his debut, during which he impressed a watching Bill Shankly.

"I knew he was a winner," said Shankly. "There are some players you watch and you really think they can play, but you are not too sure. I knew with Emlyn Hughes there was no risk."

On February 27, 1967, after discussing finances – Hughes signed for £65,000, a record fee for a full-back, and would earn £120 a week – he put pen to paper on a deal Shankly described as one of "the major signings of all time". In fact, Shankly was so keen to get his man to Liverpool he drove him there himself.

What happened next has gone down in folklore. After somebody drove into the back of Shankly's car with Hughes in it, a policeman subsequently told the Liverpool boss his vehicle wasn't roadworthy. The Scot angrily replied: "Do you know who's in this car? There sits the future England captain!"

Shankly was right, but first came a Liverpool debut, against Stoke, before a game against Newcastle United in April 1967 in which Hughes made an indelible mark. Before the match, Hughes's dad had encouraged his son to make an impact. Shankly, too, had urged his new signing to give the supporters "something to remember".

Hughes duly obliged... by rugby-tackling Albert Bennett neck-high. Hughes wasn't even booked. Instead, the incident had the Liverpool bench, and referee, in stitches. Liverpool won 3-1 and the Kop had a new hero it subsequently nicknamed 'Crazy Horse'.

Hughes was a popular figure on the terraces, as he became an irreplaceable part of a team that went on to dominate domestic and European football for the next decade. "There were three players who, through their consistency, epitomised the Liverpool way more than anyone," said John Toshack. "Ian Callaghan, Kevin Keegan and, of course, Emlyn Hughes."

Hughes started at left-back as a replacement for Willie Morgan but he loved to get forward and would cut in on his right foot. This sometimes gave wingers an advantage in one-on-one situations and prevented Hughes from crossing first-time with his left. As a result he was ushered into midfield, starting with a pre-season tour of Germany ahead of the 1967-68 season.

Here, in the centre of the pitch, he could fully express himself. His movement and energy might have confounded modern-day statisticians and he got himself into scoring positions – he loved shooting from distance and netted 49 goals in 665 games – and created space and chances for others. Some of his goals, like those against Tottenham in 1968 and Southampton in 1969, followed dynamic box-to-box movement and sweeping moves that impressed his teammates and coaching staff.

"He would always give 100 per cent," remembered Terry McDermott. "He never stopped, he was up and down the pitch, cajoling everyone."

"I don't know where he got his energy from," agreed Ian St. John. "If you could have packaged him, it would have done the whole nation of a lot of good because he never stopped."

After Don Revie attempted to take Hughes to Leeds, a move Liverpool rebuffed, Hughes enjoyed his defining season in red, in 1972-73. He played 65 games en route to a league and UEFA Cup double. It was the Reds' first league title in seven years, their first trophy in two years and the first of Hughes's career. He had been imperious.

Two years later he moved to the heart of Liverpool's defence to form a solid partnership with Phil Thompson. The duo were particularly adept at bringing the ball out of defence years before Alan Hansen made it an art form. Bob Paisley's decision to make him captain in the summer of 1973 took Hughes's Liverpool career to the next phase, although it created tension in the dressing-room.

"He would always be talking on and off the field which helped make him a good captain," said Paisley, before admitting: "He liked to be King of the Roost." Paisley's decision created a rift between Hughes and Tommy Smith that never healed. Smith's nose had been put out of joint and Paisley admitted: "As captain, Hughes was very selfish."

It was no secret that Hughes hadn't always been popular with everyone in the dressing-room. When he first joined, some senior members found his confidence misplaced. But Shankly liked it. "If they don't accept you," the Scot said, "I'll get rid of the lot of them."

Any personality conflicts were kept in-house, however and never spilled on to the field. "All that really matters is that Emlyn contributed on the pitch," said Kenny Dalglish, and Hughes more than played his part. Kevin Keegan described him as "an inspiration to the team", and Hughes oversaw an incredible spell in the club's history, first with the FA Cup in 1974, then a league and UEFA Cup double in 1976 before the ultimate prize in 1977, the European Cup.

The 1976-77 season culminated in an epic night in Rome where Liverpool overcame Borussia Moenchengladbach. Hughes had been typically committed and commanding all season and he led by example once again on that balmy night in the Italian capital. Before the game, Hughes had urged his teammates to make up for losing the FA Cup final to Manchester United days earlier and reward the thousands of Liverpool fans who had travelled to Italy. They did, and any lingering disappointment from Wembley was quickly eradicated.

After lifting the European Cup with what commentator Barry Davies described as "the smile of the season", the plaudits continued for Hughes, who won the Sportswriters' Footballer of the Year Award.

Hughes was also a key figure for England. In 1974, as Shankly had predicted to a Lancashire policeman seven years earlier, he was given the Three Lions' captaincy and he led the team on 23 of his 62 appearance under three separate England managers: Joe Mercer (who replaced Alf Ramsey), Don Revie and Ron Greenwood. Until Ian Rush broke his record, Hughes was Liverpool's most-capped player, although he never featured at a World Cup.

Liverpool regained the European title in 1978 at Wembley against Club Brugge, which proved a fitting end for Hughes before he moved to the Midlands a year later. With Wolves, he lifted the only title that had eluded him at Liverpool, the League Cup. He went on to become player-manager at Rotherham, Mansfield and Swansea City.

After he hung up his boots, Hughes was awarded an OBE in 1980, while his personality was a perfect fit for various media opportunities. Liverpool fans of a certain age will remember him as an excitable team captain on BBC quiz show *A Question of Sport*, with parents no doubt recalling tales of similar enthusiasm when Hughes was captain of Liverpool.

Supporters of all ages were united in grief when he developed a brain tumour and passed away in November 2004, aged 57. He had secured his place in Liverpool's history long before.

6 BILLY LIDDELL

LEFT MIDFIELD

BY BEN LYTTLETON

Honours First Division Championship 1947

He's in the side because… he could create and score goals at will, while his longevity with and loyalty to Liverpool, even in tough times, made him a special character

Quote "When you played against Billy, he was like a torpedo coming towards you. He had strength, skill, bravery and a big heart. He had everything that epitomised a Liverpool and Scotland player. Kenny Dalglish is the best Scottish player I've ever seen but Billy is right up there with him" – Tommy Docherty, former Scotland teammate

Greatest Moment Scoring against Everton in two FA Cup ties, the 1950 semi-final victory and then, in 1955, inspiring an upset in a 4-0 win

BILLY LIDDELL WONDERED what he had done wrong. He had arrived home on time, like always, after his Saturday night trip to the local youth-club dance in the Lanarkshire village of Townhill. But it was nearly midnight and his parents, normally in bed by ten, were waiting up for the 16-year-old.

His father asked him about the dance before his mother could keep quiet no longer.

"Right out without any preliminaries, she asked, 'Willie, how would you like to live in Liverpool?'" Liddell recounted in his biography, My Soccer Story. "I hadn't the slightest idea what the question conveyed. Football at that moment was far from my thoughts and Liverpool had never been in them at all. 'What on earth do you mean?'"

Earlier in the evening, Liverpool manager George Kay had paid Liddell's parents a visit and offered their son a contract at Anfield – but more importantly, at least for his parents, a job at respected accountants Simon, Jude and West, where he would be paid £1 per week until he signed a professional contact when he turned 17. Astonishingly, Liddell kept the job throughout his 22-year Anfield career, training full-time only during pre-season and then twice a week once the season was underway.

It was summer 1938, and Liverpool was a club in the doldrums, then in the shadow of Dixie Dean-inspired rivals Everton, with the memory of their last title success in 1923 growing ever distant. Within weeks of arriving, another Scot joined Liddell at the club: a 20-year-old called Bob Paisley, whose significance to Liverpool's history was not yet known.

When World War II broke out in September 1939, Liverpool's senior professionals joined the Territorial Army, and Liddell, a left-winger with an eye for goal, took his chance to impress in some friendly matches. The *Liverpool Echo* match report for his first appearance, against Preston, called him 'Liddle' but spoke of his "great promise" before he made people sit up and notice with goals in two 7-3 wins in wartime leagues; over Crewe Alexandra and, with a hat-trick, against Manchester City.

He was two-footed, which made him even harder to mark. It was a skill he had perfected back home when he used to deliver messages for his grandmother. "I always had a ball with me, a tennis ball or a sponge ball, and when she asked me to go to the grocers I always ran there on the left hand side of the road, pushing the ball against the wall and stopping it before it went into the road," he explained. "On the way back I would run on the same pavement so that I had to use my other foot to stop the ball going into the road."

By the time the war was over, Liddell had served with the RAF (and played a few matches while on duty abroad, including for Toronto Scottish in Canada and Linfield in Northern Ireland) and had waited eight years for his first division debut, aged 24.

He had already played nine times for Scotland, after his friend Matt Busby (who had tipped off Kay about his qualities as a teenager) urged his selection. He scored on his debut, aged 20, in a 5-4 win over England, in which Bill Shankly, then at Liverpool and another Reds legend in the making, scored the winner.

Liddell had played over 150 games for Liverpool in regional wartime divisions, but in the 1946-47 season, he took just three minutes to make his mark in his first division debut: that's when he scored his first against Chelsea, direct from a corner, and his second just after half-time, to make it 6-0 to Liverpool. The game finished 7-4.

The season's end was even more dramatic. Liverpool went into the final day in joint-second place, level on points with Wolves and Stoke. Wolves were their opponents, and with Manchester United only one point ahead with all their games played, the winner would likely win the title.

In front of a packed house at Molineux, Liddell set up captain Jack Balmer for Liverpool's opener. Albert Stubbins added a second and Liverpool won 2-1, avenging a 5-1 Anfield defeat earlier in the season. When Stoke ended up losing to Sheffield United (their rearranged game was played two weeks later), Liverpool were champions. It was Liddell's first season of league football. Little did he know, it was never going to get better than that.

When his brother Tom, a full-back, joined the Anfield playing staff in the summer of 1949, Liddell was not only still working as an accountant, but he was doing some part-time journalism too, filing reports on BBC Radio's *Sports Report* show. He was so trusted was he that he would let himself in to the BBC's Liverpool studio on Lime Street, make contact with the editors in London, send a report on what had happened at Anfield, and lock up after himself.

On the pitch, his dazzling wing-play helped Liverpool start the 1949 season with a 19-match unbeaten run. "That unbeaten run is one of my greatest Liverpool memories," he said, but it might have been even better if the referee had spotted that his 50-yard lob over Blackpool goalkeeper George Farm had bounced down off the crossbar and over the line. No goal was awarded and the game finished 0-0.

That was not the only goal that Liddell had robbed from him. In a dramatic FA Cup fifth round tie against Manchester City in 1956, Liddell struck a long-range shot in the 90th minute that flew past Bert Trautmann in goal; as the fans celebrated the strike they thought levelled up the game at 2-2, the referee walked off the pitch. He claimed he had blown the whistle for full-time before the ball went into the net, and no goal was given. It remains one of Liddell's most famous moments in a Liverpool shirt.

That 1949-50 season represented Liddell's best hope of adding to his First Division title, as his 17 goals spurred Liverpool's championship charge. But four losses in their last five games ended those dreams, and attention switched to their first appearance in an FA Cup final since 1914.

It was Liddell who had made the difference in the semi-final, with yet another strike, this time from a tight angle, to make it 2-0. "It was an absolute gift," said Liddell. "I had to shoot from the most acute angle, but I hit the ball first time with all my strength and it sped into the net like a rocket."

Arsenal were their final opponents, but there was drama even before a ball was kicked. Liverpool manager George Kay was taken ill before the game, and the board of directors that picked the team left out Paisley for Bill Jones (it was a decision that almost had significant consequences, as Paisley considered leaving the club after that snub).

The Arsenal game-plan was obvious early on: stop Liddell at all costs. After ten minutes, his Scotland team-mate Alex Forbes made a crunching challenge on Liddell that reduced the winger's impact for the rest of the match. Arsenal went on to win the final 2-0 and journalist Brian Glanville asked: "Would Arsenal have won the final if Forbes hadn't painfully fouled Liddell early in the game?"

Still, the city of Liverpool was proud of its players, and over 10,000 fans welcomed them back to the Lord Mayor's reception at the town hall. It was the last time this team would have something to celebrate for a while.

When Kay retired in 1951, the board invited Shankly for an interview to discuss replacing him. He would have taken the job but for one thing: the board still insisted on picking the team, with the manager having an advisory role.

"If I can't pick the team, what am I manager of?" asked Shankly, whose arrival at Anfield would be delayed by eight years. As Ronnie Moran, then on the club's books, noted in John Keith's biography, *Billy Liddell: The Legend Who Carried The Kop*: "If he had come a few years earlier when Billy was in his prime, things would have been very different."

As it was, 'Liddellpool', as the club was now known, was beginning to struggle. A 2-0 win over Derby on the last day of the 1951-52 season staved off relegation but in 1953-54, the team went down. Once again Liddell had top-scored but his seven goals were some way short of his previous tallies (13, 19, 15, 19).

It was at this point that Liddell became a Liverpool hero: a regular for the last eight seasons, and top scorer for the last four, he had the chance to leave the club in summer 1954 and avoid the ignominy of second-tier football, but he rejected it. He was invited to follow Everton pair Bill Higgins and Jack Hedley to play in a rebel league in Bogota, Colombia, and a £12,000 annual salary made him think about it. He later said that his twin boys, only then a few months old, were too young for him to consider moving, but his wife Phyllis said: "For various reasons, but primarily his loyalty to Liverpool, he dismissed the offer."

Instead, Liddell tore apart second-division defences, scoring 31 goals as Liverpool finished in eleventh place, its lowest ever league placing. The campaign had the odd highlight, not least the FA Cup tie against high-flying Everton. No-one gave Liverpool a chance at Goodison Park but, once again inspired by an early Liddell goal, Liverpool ran out 4-0 winners.

"It was, as so many Liverpool victories have been, Billy Liddell's game," wrote *The Sunday Express*. "This great footballer steered the team to a two-goal lead from centre-forward and when centre-half Laurie Hughes was injured in the second half, he moved to left-half. He then proved that he was Liverpool's best defender as well as their best forward. He picked off the Everton moves like ripe plums and still had time to make a goal."

Soon the records began to mount for Liddell: he marked the 400-game mark for Liverpool with a goal against Bury in December 1956 and scored on breaking Elisha Scott's Liverpool appearance record of 430 the following season. Liverpool finished in the top four of the division for four straight seasons but could not get promotion – until, that is, Shankly was belatedly appointed manager in December 1959. He would help Liverpool win the second division title in 1962.

When Shankly arrived, Liddell was 37 and used to being in and out of the side. But in his new coach, who had been his former Scotland teammate, he had a fan: "Liddell had everything," said Shankly. "He was fast, powerful, shot with either foot and his headers were like blasts from a gun. What a player!"

"There wasn't a weakness in Billy's game," added Matt Busby, another teammate who went on to be a successful manager. "He was as strong as a bull on the ball. Defenders found him a real handful, but always respected him."

By the time Liddell made his final appearance, in August 1960, he set a record for the oldest Liverpool player, aged 38 and 234 days. Fittingly, the record was broken 30 years later by another Scot, Kenny Dalglish.

He may not have played in Liverpool's most successful era, but Liddell's impact was certainly significant: especially in that debut top-flight season, which ended with the title, and his first in the second division. Take away his 31 goals and Liverpool may have been staring a place in the third division and then who knows what may have happened to the club?

In all, Liddell played 492 league games and scored 215 goals. Imagine how many more that might have been had the war not curtailed the start of his career. As reserve goalkeeper Tommy Lawrence, who was often on the end of Liddell's swerving shots when he stayed behind for extra training when he joined the players twice a week, put it: "Usually if Billy didn't play, Liverpool didn't win."

7 STEVEN GERRARD

CENTRAL MIDFIELD

BY CHRIS BASCOMBE

Honours Champions League 2005; FA Cup 2001, 2006; League Cup 2001, 2003, 2012, UEFA Cup 2001, UEFA Super Cup 2001, 2005; Community Shield 2001, 2006

In the side because... he is the complete, modern midfielder, a leader who has delivered when it mattered most to his club, particularly during an era when there has been a dearth of world class talent at Anfield

Quote "None of the players who've played alongside Stevie would dispute he's the best the club has ever had, and I would hope none of the managers would either" – Jamie Carragher

Greatest moment Lifting the Champions League trophy in Istanbul after inspiring a second-half comeback against AC Milan, having earlier been the chief reason Liverpool qualified for the competition and progressed through the group stages

STEVEN GERRARD WAS not having one of his better games. On the periphery of the action, possibly trying too hard, occasionally over-hitting passes which were usually routine, and unable to manoeuvre himself into areas to inflict maximum damage on the opposing defence.

Then, 25 yards from goal, the ball rolled invitingly into range of his right foot and he let rip. It flew past Antonios Nikopolidis, prompting the kind of Anfield eruption which would cause the iconic stadium to tremble again over the next few months, but only as an aftershock of this single, defining moment.

It was 9.26pm on December 8, 2004 and it was a shot that was heard around the world, irreversibly changing the course of Liverpool history, setting the path for the rest of Gerrard's club career.

Despite numerous temptations, and a couple of moments when his feet felt they'd been doused in itching powder, this was the night that bound Liverpool and Gerrard together forever.

In simple terms, it meant Liverpool defeated Olympiakos 3-1 in their final Champions League group game, winning by the two goals required to qualify for the last sixteen. They would go on to win the competition during one of the most improbable cup comebacks, climaxed by an incomprehensible final which is now simply referred by its venue: 'Istanbul'.

Gerrard would lead the revival against AC Milan the following May, too, but in the now much analysed and occasionally revised history of that season, the Olympiakos strike – captured for posterity by a gloriously partisan cry of "You beauty" by the Sky TV commentator and ex-Everton striker Andy Gray – is too often overlooked. In the context of Gerrard's career, and Liverpool's enduring place in European football, it was the catalyst for all that followed.

Volumes have already been written and more city libraries will be filled with tales about tactical masterplans, half-time talks, average players elevating themselves to hitherto unseen heights and lung-busting Anfield atmospheres, but ultimately it came down to the Liverpool supporter from Huyton's streetwise Bluebell Estate; a player who not only lived the dream of playing for his boyhood club, but has proven himself capable under the severest pressure to fulfil the expectations of an insisting fan base.

To understand why this rates as the most important goal in Liverpool's modern history – and why it reinforces Gerrard's position in all-time Anfield Best XI – it is worth considering where the club was heading prior to the captain's intervention against the Greeks.

24 hours before the Olympiakos visit, Gerrard delivered a provocative warning to Liverpool, issued with the kind of brutal honesty which is unpalatable to parochial ears. He said if Liverpool continued to fail to compete at the highest level at home and abroad, he'd move on.

"I'm captain, I'm a local lad, and the fans obviously don't want to see their best players leave so I'm in an incredibly difficult position," he said. "I know if I go some fans will understand but others will be really upset and turn against me. I want to win things with Liverpool more than anything, that would give me most pleasure. But I want to be in the title race for real next season. I really hope by the end of the season the club can show me that they are as ambitious as I am. If not, then I will have to think again in the summer."

These comments marked a symbolic change in Liverpool's status. Since the arrival of Bill Shankly in 1959, Liverpool only ever allowed their best players to leave on the club's terms. Now – just a few months after Michael Owen left for Real Madrid – another of their youth products was considering quitting because he could not foresee success in the near future. Chelsea had been trying to sign Gerrard for two years, and Liverpool's captain resisted the overtures amid promises a new Anfield regime would compete for the honours he craved.

In the previous season, Gerrard's consecutive man-of-the-match performances allowed Gerard Houllier's reign as manager to end with the consolation of Champions League qualification. But four months into the reign of new manager Rafa Benitez, there were fears things were deteriorating.

Liverpool were seventh, already 15 points behind Chelsea and nine behind their city rivals Everton. With Liverpool's exit from the Champions League seemingly inevitable, Gerrard was not in the mood for sugar-coated diplomacy on the eve of the Olympiakos visit.

Players and managers are often described as being at the crossroads of a career. The Olympiakos night was Liverpool's ultimate *Sliding Doors* moment. If events had turned out differently that evening, the club would not have spent the summer of 2005 swimming in the pool of euphoria after a fifth European Cup, but drowning in the depression at the loss of its iconic, home-grown star.

Gerrard would have joined Chelsea, Benitez would not have had the golden mark on his CV that bought him instant legendary status (Liverpool finished fifth in the league that season) and he'd also have been denied the following season's FA Cup win – which included an almost carbon copy 'Olympiakos goal' from Gerrard to deny West Ham victory in the last minute.

There is a danger of sounding clichéd by recalling such frequent *Roy of the Rovers* moments, but the scripts have been comic book. Gerrard has often been described as being too individualistic in his style, but only by those who either refuse to acknowledge the mediocrity he has been surrounded by for prolonged periods of his Liverpool career, or simply never experienced enough of those dire and dour games rescued by a

Gerrard goal or assist.

On several occasions, it has only been Gerrard's individual brilliance that has elevated Liverpool from an average mid-table side into one that was not only able to hang on to European qualification but actually win the most prestigious competition.

Gerrard is Liverpool's modern-day Billy Liddell, a dedicated one-club man capable of performing in any position whose loyalty has come at the expense of a multitude of honours he could have won elsewhere. The Chelsea rejection (twice) was played out in public. In private, despite several formal approaches, Real Madrid and Inter Milan were also politely informed a bid would not lead to a transfer as Gerrard chose to commit his entire career to Liverpool.

Those pre-Olympiakos quotes demonstrate another factor separating Gerrard from other Anfield greats. Being a Liverpudlian in the Liverpool team brings additional pressure as the demand from supporters can be debilitating. The empathy in victory adds to the euphoria, but in leaner or more turbulent times the Merseyside contingent within the squad is more likely to feel besieged, as if they in particular have let the club and its support down. As well as an exceptional footballer, Gerrard has often been expected to be a club spokesman or even resemble a social worker, helping to maintain the psychological well-being of a community whose mood is dictated by footballing success.

His medal haul is unjustly thin, although it is worth noting he has won every club honour except the Premier League title, scoring in Champions League, UEFA Cup, FA Cup and League Cup Final victories. He said winning the European Cup once with Liverpool meant more than winning it ten times anywhere else. The same would apply to the club's long lost friend, the Premier League, which remains so elusive. On his debut in 1999, Gerrard would never have believed he'd still be pursuing the title 13 years later.

Those of us who've covered the club during the entirety of his career can recall their first sighting of the gloriously nurtured talent from the Anfield youth ranks. Liverpool's Academy under former youth director Steve Heighway was notorious for stamping out with military force any hype surrounding young players, and he was initially able to contain the amount of attention on Gerrard because of a series of injuries in his youth.

That changed as the first team beckoned. Shortly after his appointment, initially as joint-manager, Gerard Houllier wasted no time promoting the youngster to the senior set-up.

"I was told by Peter Robinson [Anfield's former chief executive] when I joined Liverpool I would not need to worry about signing a world class midfielder because of the young player we had coming through the ranks," recalled Houllier.

Houllier took a paternal approach to the midfielder in public, but privately he never disguised his enthusiasm. France's Academy in Clairefontaine had yielded its golden period while Houllier was Technical Director of their FA and he believed Gerrard compared favourably with those who'd just emerged to win the World Cup and European Championships.

It was impossible for anyone covering Liverpool Football Club not to feel empowered by the knowing vibes surrounding the superkid about to fulfil his potential.

I recall my own giddiness when a member of Liverpool's Academy staff, Steve Cavanagh, urged me to watch an Under 18 match and closely observe the performance of 'this unbelievable lad we've got coming through'. At 17, Gerrard appeared to possess the range of passing of Jan Molby, the intimidating presence of Graeme Souness and running capacity and goal threat from midfield of the marauding Terry McDermott.

After seeing him play for the first time, it was one of those occasions where you skipped back to the office believing you'd just been made privy to the greatest of footballing secrets.

Teammates became less discreet in their praise as the race to claim most credit for 'spotting' Gerrard intensified. Both Michael Owen and Jamie Redknapp predicted he would be the star of the Premier League before he'd made two back-to-back starts. They were rapidly shown to be perceptive judges, but it was already the equivalent of backing the winning horse in the

Grand National after it had been run.

Whether at right back – Gerrard's first Merseyside derby was a man-of-the-match performance in the defensive role – right midfield, a second striker or his preferred all-action central midfield role, he could excel.

At first, his only barrier was the persistent muscular injuries as he grew up, delaying the speed with which he could become a regular. By the 1999-2000 season, he was already Liverpool's best player. He made his England debut at the end of that campaign, beginning a career that belatedly brought international captaincy. Such was Houllier's confidence in him, he sold his captain Paul Ince because he knew Gerrard was a natural successor.

The thrilling moments have been relentlessly recurrent, but a personal favourite came in the early stages of that campaign.

Ince had not taken his sale well, publicly criticising Houllier and assistant Phil Thompson for moving him on and Liverpool travelled to Middlesbrough – Ince's new club – a few weeks after the ex-skipper's public attack on the new management team.

In the first minute, teenager Gerrard thrust himself into a 50-50 tackle with his former captain and emerged with the ball. On the bench, Houllier must have felt the sense of vindication, his youngster's venomous tenacity as inspiring as many of the goal exploits that followed. Although his pride was understandably wounded, deep down Ince must have understood the validity of the decision to sell him to allow Gerrard to assume more responsibility – something he has had to get used to ever since.

During his thirteen years in the senior side, there have been only two genuinely top class Liverpool teams that have not utterly depended on him.

The first was the 2001 Treble-winning side, when playing alongside the canny Gary McAllister coincided with another rapid improvement in Gerrard's all-round game.

By 2003, Gerrard was the club's captain. An initially self-confident, but often withdrawn character, his levels of self-awareness had grown with every year. When he spoke, he did so with the gravitas of a player aware of his importance and trying to negotiate the fine line between being a trustworthy, loyal lieutenant and advocate for change when it was needed. Whatever Liverpool's toils were off the park – and there have been far too many - Gerrard has continued to perform on it.

The only other side which was not wholly dependant on Gerrard was that which almost won the title under Benitez in 2008-09. With Xabi Alonso, Javier Mascherano and Fernando Torres flourishing, Gerrard was finally able to share the responsibility, excelling in a role behind the star striker as Benitez was briefly able to build as a team complementary to disparate talents rather than reliant on one player.

The swift disintegration of that line-up due to the off-field politics the Liverpool captain found reprehensible created a period of Anfield self-destruction will always be one of Gerrard's greatest regrets.

After seeing Alonso, Mascherano and Torres leave, the lure of a final pay day elsewhere must have been strong for Gerrard, but he opted to try to assist the succession of recent managerial appointments. To those with no loyalty to Liverpool, Gerrard's decisions to stay would have been inexplicable.

Jamie Carragher once said of Gerrard he will not be fully appreciated until he is no longer playing for Liverpool. There remains merit in this argument, with many Liverpool supporters preferring to give most credit to those who've overseen Gerrard's triumphs rather than acknowledge it has often been the player who has been the making of the manager as much as the coach moulding the player.

It's hard to recall anyone whose individual contribution has been so pivotal to a club so often while hearing a sequence of coaches assume the credit for facilitating his success. In 2005, especially, Gerrard was to Liverpool what Diego Maradona was to Argentina's World Cup winning team of 1986. Arguing Gerrard shone in the Champions League triumph due to anything but his own inspirational brilliance is the equivalent to Argentina's winning coach in Mexico, Carlos Bilardo, claiming Maradona's dribble against England was a consequence of a perfectly structured tactical plan.

Under any manager, in any era, Gerrard would have been exceptional and there is a strong case for arguing he would have achieved far more had he decided to move on at the peak of his powers. The fact he stayed at Liverpool in an era of temptation adds to the legend.

Ultimately, what matters is Gerrard's imprint on some of the most astounding Liverpool victories in a career which now prompts a regular debate as to whether he or Kenny Dalglish is the greatest to ever wear the red shirt.

It is a career which is still continuing in the hope of winning the Premier League title to ensure once he can finish with a deserved, final satisfactory flourish.

One of the Liverpool supporters' most evocative banners during their European campaigns depicted Gerrard as Russell Crowe's character Maximus in the film *Gladiator*. "What we do in life, echoes in eternity," it proclaims.

When Gerrard calls time on his playing career and replays his array of history-making goals, there will be no finer epitaph.

8 GRAEME SOUNESS

CENTRAL MIDFIELD

BY LEO MOYNIHAN

Honours First Division Championship 1979, 1980, 1982, 1984, 1984; European Cup 1978, 1981, 1984; League Cup 1981, 1982, 1983, 1984; Charity Shield 1980, 1981, 1983

He's in the side because... he's the complete midfielder who gave some of Liverpool's greatest ever teams both style and grit

Quote "Most midfields are made up of a buzzing type of player, a cruncher for winning the ball, and a spreader for the passing. Souness is all three" – Bob Paisley

Greatest moment Lifting the European Cup in Rome after beating Roma. Without Souness's leadership qualities, it wouldn't have happened

SOME OF THE younger, less steely characters in the squad are a bit overawed. They are good players, of course they are, but this is a test of anyone's mettle and nerves are filling the dressing-room.

A few of them turned on their hotel televisions four hours before kick-off to see a stadium already three-quarters full. The noise is now building, flares are lit, and the locals are ready.

This is Rome in 1984. The European Cup Final is soon to kick off, the opponents are Roma and in a city where the locals have long marvelled at the persecution of their sporting visitors, the atmosphere is becoming biblical in its intensity.

Graeme Souness is not a player or a man familiar with intimidation (if the Christians who were thrown to the lions in this very city had been cut from his stock, it would have been the lions cowering in fear) and despite the volume raising outside, the captain decides steps must be taken.

"Let's go for a walk," says Souness to his team. The players follow him through a wall of boos, thinking they will take solace near their own band of eager supporters. No chance.

"Now let's walk right around in front of their lot," says Souness. 'That'll shock 'em."

Eyebrows are raised – as is the volume – but once again they follow. "Their fans hated us for it," recalls the centre-back Mark Lawrenson. "It showed them that they didn't intimidate us. Souey was loving it, but it wasn't pleasant."

That was Souness: uber-confident, brash, confrontational and brilliant. The 'This is Anfield' sign might offer visitors a symbolic reminder of where and whom opponents are playing but between 1978 and 1984, it was an early tackle from Souness that rattled the point home.

Signed from Middlesbrough for £352,000 – a then record fee between two English clubs – Souness was seen as the perfect 'new' midfielder. Yes, the club were champions of Europe but as ever at Anfield, laurels were not there to be rested upon.

Ian Callaghan, a player with more appearances in Liverpool's red than any other, had been wonderful in the centre of Bob Paisley's midfield but his 20-year tenure at the club was coming to an end. In Souness, Paisley saw a dynamic future.

Born in Edinburgh, Souness began his career in 1968 in London as an apprentice at Tottenham Hotspur. Part of a successful youth team, the young Souness – already showing sings of the confidence that would one day wreak havoc on teams at home and abroad – became disgruntled with how hard it was to make the step up.

Yes, Spurs under Bill Nicholson were a top team; yes, in the early 1970s they were good enough to win European honours and yes, their midfield housed England internationals such as Alan Mullery and Martin Peters, but to the teenage Souness, he was good enough and he had questions that he wanted answering.

A knock on Nicholson's door and a few choice words from both parties were enough to end Souness's time at White Hart Lane. He was only 19 but his career needed a re-think before it had even begun. A spell on loan at Montreal Olympique in the North American Soccer League was a success before being signed by Middlesbrough, where soon he would not only get his chance but would blossom under manager Jack Charlton.

Boro might have been playing Second Division football – not a place he saw himself – but with Souness dictating their play, they immediately won promotion and the Scot began to get noticed.

Bob Paisley was among the admirers and in January 1978 he made his move. Souness had his discipline problems and was fond of his nightlife but that wouldn't deter the Liverpool boss (it wasn't as if he was managing a team of monks at Anfield!).

Souness was ecstatic by the possibility and grabbed the pen to sign the contract immediately. The club drove him home in a limousine (this was the life he expected and deserved) and days later he was making his debut in a 1-0 win at West Bromwich Albion.

On his first day at Liverpool's training-ground at Melwood, Souness strolled in and confidently asked the then alpha-male at the club, Tommy Smith, if he could use his hair-dryer. Smith turned to Phil Neal and said, "Everyone's allowed one mistake." From then on, Souness used his own.

He had hit the big time. The superstar teammates, the limos, and the hotel instead of the digs he was used to when joining a new club. These were the trappings of fame that came with signing for the best team in Europe but for the extrovert 25-year-old, they brought temptations too. Temptations that can tarnish a player's reputation.

"This was the start of the third period of my life during which I very nearly managed to wreck my own career," Souness later admitted. "I lived [in the hotel] for nine months and it was then I earned the nickname of 'Champagne Charlie'. The routine was quickly established.

"I would train at Melwood, go back for lunch and a few beers, get involved in a session at the cocktail bar, sleep between 4pm and 7pm, and then crawl back down for dinner. If that became a little too boring there was always a club open somewhere, where they were only too happy to have a Liverpool player gracing their bar or the dance floor."

Kenny Dalglish had signed for the club the previous summer and was still living in the same hotel with his young family and would joke with his neighbour; asking him to bring him breakfast on his way in from another night out.

But Souness wasn't wrapped in cotton wool by Paisley. This was Liverpool and as long as the work was put in at Melwood and games won at Anfield, the staff were happy. Soon, so were the fans.

Six weeks after his arrival, Souness faced Dave Sexton's Manchester United at Anfield. United had stopped Liverpool from winning the treble the previous May and had already beaten Paisley's team at Old Trafford that season. Almost 50,000 fans crammed into the stadium, the vast majority baying for revenge. They got it.

On 39 minutes, Souness found some room just inside United's half. He looked up, sprayed the ball to the right wing to an eager Terry McDermott who carried it forward. This was Souness the player. He liked to admire his reflection and prune his hair off the pitch but he wasn't going to admire his pass and he quickly continued forward. The United defence, occupied by Liverpool's strikers, backed off. Souness took the space on the edge of their box and demanded McDermott pull the ball back.

The cross was lofted up and at the Anfield Road end, using his less trusted left foot, Souness smashed the ball past Paddy Roche in the United goal from 18 yards and high into the net. It was goal of that season and a moment that signified the arrival of a hero. "I was on the Anny Road that night," said playwright and Liverpool fanatic Dave Kirby. "Souness gave me a smile as big as Liberace."

Liverpool didn't win the First Division title in that first season but with Souness bedded into the centre of their midfield, they reached a second successive European Cup Final, where they would face the Belgian champions Bruges at Wembley.

It was a tight, frustrating night for Liverpool. Bruges offered little space or attacking intent and it was going to take something special to break the deadlock, but with 26 minutes left, Souness received the ball on the edge of the box.

Immediately he was set upon by a horde of defenders but he kept his cool, dropped the shoulder, made a bit of space and played in a deft pass for Kenny Dalglish, who with similar panache dinked it over the onrushing Birger Jensen in the Bruges goal. The trophy was coming back to Anfield.

It was an exceptional pass from Souness. He had already proved himself up for any physical challenge and goals like the crashing volley against United had underlined the dynamite in his boots, but this was another side to his game; subtle and clever. Souness was proving himself the ultimate midfielder.

That goal at Wembley also cemented a relationship with Dalglish that would bring so much success. Rightly so, much is made of the Dalglish and Ian Rush combination that brought so many goals but Souness would also dovetail with Dalglish, the perfect bridge between midfield and attack.

Dalglish had been wary of Souness at first. He had been asked to room with him on Scotland duty before Souness arrived at Anfield but would often stay away from the room, coming in when he knew Souness was asleep. Once club teammates, Souness asked Dalglish what that was all about. The Glaswegian admitted that what with the hair-dryer, the continental colognes and the bushy moustache that, "I thought you were bit of a poof, big man."

With those misunderstandings cleared up, the pair thrived. Dalglish would drop into deep positions, taking concerned defenders with him and Souness, as such an intelligent player, would know when to bomb on and exploit the gaps left behind. This was simple, effective football dependent on good teamwork and at its hub was Souness.

The 1978-79 team at Anfield is regarded by many purists as the club's best ever. Souness soldiered the centre of the midfield and despite the brilliance of Terry McDermott beside him, the Scot managed to be the playmaker, a goal-threat *and* offer an often bored defence (they conceded only 16 league goals that campaign) his granite-like protection.

The league championship was won again the following season and the European Cup once more in 1981. In that European campaign, Souness put on a master class of long-range shooting with a hat-trick against CSKA Sofia at Anfield and by now his status on the Kop was set in stone.

Souness was very much the present and the future of the club but Paisley had realised after the European Cup win in Paris that the team's past was catching up with it. Like any great manager, the Durham man knew that tough decisions needed to be taken and older players, however great, had to be replaced.

Half-way through the next season, with the team struggling in mid-table, he also saw that in

Souness he had the perfect leader, a man who would captain a younger, fresher team and so despite lifting that European trophy just months before, Phil Thompson was asked to give up the armband.

"One day, at half-time during a dodgy performance at Villa Park, Bob asked Thommo if maybe the captaincy was not a bit too much for him," recalled Souness. "Phil, a proud Liverpudlian who treasured the captaincy, gave a very abrupt reply. Bob did not like that one bit and flew back at him. It was a rare sight and, a few days later, I was leaning against a goalpost helping to collect balls at shooting practice session when he asked me how I would feel about the captaincy.

"I knew that that was what I wanted and I told him that if it was offered I would take it, and sure enough at the next match at Swansea I was captain. It was a great thrill and a great honour even though it ended any pretence of friendship between Phil Thompson and me. He took it as a personal affront and it was a long, long time before he would say even hello to me."

Souness wasn't the type to let broken friendships deter him and under his stewardship on the pitch, Liverpool rallied and with a team that included a young Rush, Ronnie Whelan and Craig Johnston went on an amazing winning streak to take the title with a game to spare.

Paisley was drawn to Souness as a captain due to his unerring will to win but also he had a swagger and an arrogance that the manager felt would inspire the youngsters around him. "It wouldn't surprise me if Graeme tossed up before a game with a gold plated credit card rather than a coin," joked Paisley.

The last game of that season was at Souness's former club Middlesbrough. The team travelled to the North-East on the morning of the evening game, checked into their hotel rooms and got ready for a pre-match sleep. Souness had other ideas.

He knocked on doors, rounded up players and led them to a pub he knew well where they sat and drank pints of lager until the captain suggested they get back before first-team coach and disciplinarian Ronnie Moran did his rounds.

"Needless to say, I was far from my best against Middlesbrough," recalls Rush. "The lunchtime session didn't seem to effect Graeme too much, though. He dominated midfield and was running about as if he had never been to the pub at all. My performance was so lax during the first half that he came up to me and said, 'You are allowed to kick the ball, you know!'"

Led astray off the pitch, Souness demanded similar attention on it. "I remember scoring a fifth goal in a game against Luton," said Rush. "I took all the congratulations off the lads, but not off Graeme. 'Go and get a sixth' he barked."

In 1983, Liverpool won the title again but it

was after another League Cup win that he chose to be a follower, sending Paisley up in front of him to collect the trophy on what was the great manager's last game in charge at Wembley.

It was a fine gesture but Souness – thanks to his winning goal against Everton – lifted the trophy himself the following season in a campaign that would see him raise three cups.

The 1983-84 Treble at Liverpool was to be Souness's last as he was having his head turned by foreign admirers – but he wasn't going to go without leaving his mark on everything, including the odd player's face.

The league title was won at a canter but it was the European Cup that saw him and his team show incredible character on their road to Rome. Every away leg was won in trying circumstances, with none tougher than the semi-final against Dinamo Bucharest.

The first leg at Anfield had been a tight affair (won by a very rare headed goal from Sammy Lee) but the visitors left incensed after Souness was accused of throwing a sly right-hook onto the chin of the Romanian midfielder Lica Moliva, breaking his jaw in the process.

The Romanians vowed revenge and it was with some trepidation that some of the players landed in the communist state. "We're traveling to the stadium when these soldiers all ring the bus, looking for Souey," remembered Lawrenson.

"Here are these guys with Kalashnikovs peering into the window to find the perpetrator and we've nowhere to hide. Eventually they found him and one soldier puts his finger across his neck as if he was cutting his throat. Souey just shrugged his shoulders. He loved it."

Warming up was just as hostile. Souness, who played keepy-uppy in front of the soldiers and fans baying for revenge, went on to have an absolute stormer of a game in a very hostile midfield and Liverpool left having won the match 2-1.

To Souness then, the cauldron of that Roman cup final was nothing. Against midfielders of the calibre of Falcao and Bruno Conti, Souness went toe-to-toe, tackling, passing, urging his teammates on. The game was won on penalties (Souness, socks around his ankles, calmly slotted in his effort) and he had his hands on that famously big-eared trophy.

Souness had played 359 games and scored 55 goals but this was his last act in a Liverpool shirt before a big-money transfer to Sampdoria and he would – from the terraces and within the dressing-room – be missed.

"His desire and will to win was absolute and he radiated this to every other player in the side, urging us to bigger and better things," gushed Rush. "When the going got tough, Graeme was tougher than tough. He led by example and such was his commitment and fight, we players were incited to battle harder, too, not least because we didn't want to be the subject of his wrath after the game."

Souness would return for an ultimately ill-fated spell as manager but it is as their dynamic and brilliant midfielder that supporters of a certain age will always remember him.

Younger fans know and talk of Patrick Vieira, Roy Keane, Paul Scholes and their own Steven Gerrard as the ultimate Premier League midfield maestros but in Souness, Liverpool once had all those players in one stylish, effervescent and very hard man.

9 JOHN BARNES

RIGHT MIDFIELD

BY PAUL TOMKINS

Honours First Division Championship 1988, 1990; FA Cup 1989, 1992; League Cup 1995; Charity Shield 1989, 1990, 1991

In the team because... he is the most exciting player in the club's history and in terms of attacking ability, he was the complete package

Quote "Players like John Barnes come along just once in a lifetime" – Tom Finney

Greatest moment The entire 1987-88 season, when he added a dimension Liverpool had never seen before

AN OUTSTRETCHED LEFT boot, planted on halfway-line chalk. A perfectly executed block-tackle. A spin into space, and half of the Anfield pitch opens up. New boy John Barnes is away, running at the defence of table-toppers QPR. The ease with which, having approached the edge of the box, he jinks to his left, past a lunging tackle, transforms a great skill into something effortless.

But it is the way he drags the ball to his right, and somehow readjusts his balance, that defines one of the greatest goals the famous stadium has ever seen.

It defies belief, not least because he somehow manages to accelerate in the process. England international Terry Fenwick, a Tussauds waxwork in blue-and-white hoops, is bypassed. England full-back Paul Parker slides in, but is not quick enough. England goalkeeper David Seaman – beaten by a Barnes curler into the top corner earlier in the half – is left helpless again, as the Reds' number 10, with his right instep, nonchalantly slips the ball beneath the man in green.

John Barnes had impressed in the early part of his debut season, but this is the moment the Jamaican-born winger arrives. The Kop, who had been deprived of the chance to see the new man due to a collapsed sewer that saw the stadium closed until mid-September, were finally seeing his genius first-hand.

His home debut had been against Oxford United, and he scored a fine free-kick. Liverpool then beat Charlton, Derby and Portsmouth at home – Kenny Dalglish's side scoring eleven goals in a trio of victories – although Barnes was not amongst the scorers. But then came that QPR game, and an idol was born. In his 1999 autobiography he noted that it was the most memorable moment of his Liverpool career.

For the next four years Barnes terrorised English defences, scoring 75 times in all competitions. His versatility was showcased in the way he went on to excel at centre-forward in 1989-90 (having ended his time at Watford in the role), and when, after an Achilles tendon injury in 1991 sapped his acceleration, he later rebuilt his career as a deep-lying central midfielder, recycling possession and, at the age of 32, earning an England recall in that role.

It's fair to say that John Barnes was viewed with suspicion when, in June 1987, Dalglish signed the Watford winger for £900,000; a hefty fee coming at a time when Liverpool had never broken the £1m barrier (that happened a month later, with the arrival of Peter Beardsley).

There were no black players at Liverpool or Everton at the time, and it was an era where racism from the terraces was still rife. To make matters worse, Barnes's heart had been set on a move to Italy, at the time the leading league in world football.

While Watford contacted Tottenham, Liverpool and Manchester United, the player's agent, Athole Still, was hawking his client to leading Serie A clubs. It was widely known that a video had been produced to try and seduce AC Milan and Juventus, but only Sampdoria and Verona were interested. A quote appeared in the Liverpool Echo saying that Barnes wanted to move abroad or stay in London.

There were also doubts about a player moving from a long-ball, low-expectations side with no great top-flight history, and whether he could adapt to the pressure and style of play at Liverpool. Those fears, expressed far and wide, were utterly misplaced.

Barnes was nothing short of sensational. Despite his solid frame (before it became more – how shall I put it? – meaty), he glided across the pitch, moving with grace and poise. And for a silky-skilled winger, he had end product. He got into positions with pace, power and skill, and then found the killer pass or the inch-perfect cross: how many times did John Aldridge have to just nod in on the six-yard box, so delightful was the curve and weight on the centre?

In an era before assists were recorded, by viewing all the league goals from the late 1980s and early 1990s, it's clear that Barnes got into double figures for assist in each of those first four campaigns.

Despite a full decade at Anfield, did Barnes ever perform better than in his first year? It was a season of constant mazy dribbles, astute passes and 15 league goals. Or did the shock and awe of that first season create a fantasy, where anything less than beating several men and providing a cool finish produced disappointment? Had he painted himself into a corner of perfection?

By his second season he already seemed a fraction heavier, and scored eight times in the top division. But this bulk and strength, allied to pace and quick feet, made him a hugely effective centre-forward, and he featured there on occasions in 1989-90, when he won his second Football Writers' Player Of The Year award, after finishing the league's top scorer with 22 goals, and adding six more in the cups.

In those first four years, he averaged more than 15 goals a season but that dropped to less than four a season for the next six years, to highlight how his game had altered. Still, in ten straight seasons – with Watford and Liverpool, between 1981 and 1991 – he never registered fewer than 13 goals in a season, and overall he managed 108 goals in 407 Liverpool appearances.

To put Barnes's scoring record into perspective, Ryan Giggs, another prodigious winger whose game was reinvented in a similar way, but who has spent his entire career at a dominant club, up to summer 2012 had scored 163 goals in 909 club games; by contrast, Barnes, in his 19-year career, scored 35 more in 128 fewer matches.

One hallmark of greatness is just how good the player was at his peak, just how brightly he burned. Another is the duration of his excellence; precisely how long the flame lasted. Barnes had ten years in Liverpool's first team, but it was the first four that mark him out as a legend.

The question for such players becomes whether or not their legacy is ruined by their merely human years. Is that perfection blemished, or can you place those vintage years into a glass display cabinet, and label them untouchable? Had Barnes stayed as a struggling winger, short of the old pace, he may well have eroded some of those memories. The fact that he managed several more years in a completely different role – performances that, on their own, would not see him in this XI – probably helps, because he wasn't damaging the memory of Barnes the winger.

Perhaps the hardest question to answer is just how Barnes would be remembered had he arrived in 1994 as a portly possession master. Would people see a Xavi-esque ball retainer, whose appreciation of time, space and the weight of a pass, kept Liverpool ticking over with metronomic rhythm, or would he have been viewed as a lazy, tackle-dodging midfielder who failed to burst with dynamism into the box?

Perhaps it didn't help that he was partnered with Jamie Redknapp, who was brave in always wanting the ball, but like Barnes, not great at fighting to win it. By the time manager Roy Evans plumped for midfield steel, it was Barnes, now almost 34, who made way for Paul Ince.

If those first four seasons saw a '10 out of 10' player, he added six more as a 'seven' or 'eight'. Despite 224 games for the Reds after his Achilles injury dulled his verve, the legendary status was confirmed by his first 178.

To be recognised as great, players are often expected to be part of a successful side, and there's no doubt that Barnes, at his best, fits the bill, because he elevated an excellent Liverpool side to a sensational one.

His less remarkable incarnation was in keeping with the club as a whole: when his Achilles snapped in 1991, Liverpool's demise was hastened. Due to the post-Heysel ban, Barnes also missed out on playing in the European Cup, which, through no fault of his own, left one major question unanswered.

Most greats lit up that particular stage. That said, he was the undoubted creative light in what Tom Finney described in 1988 as the best English side he'd ever seen, and it almost didn't need that highest-level participation. At the time, only AC Milan, whose first of three European Cups in six seasons was still a year away, looked capable of matching the Reds.

As an individual, albeit one finely attuned to the team's needs, Barnes had it all. He displayed skill without excess, flair without showboating. There were nutmegs and drag-backs aplenty, but perhaps as a result of Graham Taylor's hard-line Watford drilling – and the military discipline of his colonel father – the aim was always to be as direct as possible: get into the heart of the opposition box, or to the byline to deliver a cross.

If space was tight, and there were three men around him, then the tricks might come out, but only to work himself free. Nothing was overdone or overblown. No blind alleys were wound down. Nothing was done to humiliate an opponent. He'd shift the ball one way, then the other, and the balance was perfect. The acceleration would do the rest.

Barnes was also excellent in the air. Every headed goal seemed to be met with the commentator noting "a rare headed goal by John

Barnes", yet he got several each season. His upper body strength was immense, aided by the thighs of a bodybuilder. Matthew Le Tissier (himself no lightweight) once remarked that, in going shoulder-to-shoulder, he just bounced off Barnes.

In his 1996 autobiography, Ian Rush described Barnes as: "A beautifully balanced runner, who could glide past defenders seemingly effortlessly. He also had great vision and the ability to split defences with one telling pass [...] But his greatest asset of all – and one that a lot of spectators have never fully appreciated – has been his sheer physical strength. When he had the ball he could hold off two, or even three, defenders with his power. At his devastating best, Barnes was a player of true world class."

In 2006, John Barnes was voted fifth in the official Liverpool website's '100 Players Who Shook the Kop'. Had serious injury not robbed him of one of his greatest assets, he would surely have ranked even higher.

10 KENNY DALGLISH

FORWARD

BY LEO MOYNIHAN

Honours First Division Championship 1979, 1980, 1982, 1983, 1984, 1986; FA Cup 1986, 1989; European Cup 1978, 1981, 1984; League Cup 1981, 1982, 1983, 1984; European Super Cup 1977; Charity Shield 1977, 1979, 1980, 1982, 1986, 1988, 1989

In the team because... he's quite simply the greatest to ever wear Liverpool's red. He's not called 'The King' for nothing.

Quote "I just hoped that after the trials and tribulations of my early years in management, someone up high would smile on me and guide my hand. My plea was answered when we got Kenny Dalglish. What a player, what a great professional!" – Bob Paisley

Best Moment The perfectly-executed goal at Chelsea to win the league title in 1986. In that moment Dalglish was manager, player, match-winner and hero

AN EIGHT YEAR-OLD boy runs into his house and up the stairs. His knees and face are muddied from a day's football in the park. He'd still be playing but for the boring matter of his tea and a good night's sleep.

Tomorrow will bring another marathon match, and once again he'll dribble like John Barnes, tackle like Steve McMahon and score like Ian Rush. These are the boy's heroes, the current stars of the Liverpool team he adores.

The boy gets to his room and in walks his dad, with a new poster. Which one of the current crop will it be? "Here you go, son," says the eager dad. "Kenny Dalglish is the best player who ever played for Liverpool. He's the man. Get him up on your wall." So up he went.

That boy was Steven Gerrard and like so many kids of the past, present and future, to him Kenny Dalglish will always be the man.

Whatever the generation, to those who see their regular trip to Anfield as more pilgrimage than pleasure, Dalglish is more than a mere poster. Through hard work, infinite skill and by just getting what makes those fans tick, Dalglish is part of the fabric of the club. Like the Kop, Bill Shankly, Bob Paisley and You'll Never Walk Alone, Dalglish is immersed in the place and the place is immersed in him.

What a player. Every now and then, along comes a footballer that makes grown men simply puff out their cheeks and look at each other as if to say, "Did you see that?" To Bob Paisley, the man who signed him, Dalglish was the greatest to ever wear Liverpool's red, but he might also be described as the greatest to ever hail from these shores.

That honour makes for a good pub debate but if the hostelry is within a corner kick of Anfield, the debate won't last long. Dalglish is the king. A man who scored goals and made goals; and whose infectious smile brought on thousands more.

Signed in 1977 for £440,000 (on his Liverpool debut in the Charity Shield, Manchester United fans sang, "What a waste of money!") he might have joined a decade earlier. Dalglish's first ever glimpse of Melwood came just weeks after England had won the World Cup when he came for a trial.

He impressed in a 'B' team match against Southport and Bill Shankly was keen to take things further but the ultra-shy Glaswegian was reluctant to leave the familiar surroundings of home.

"During my trial I wanted to get some autographs," Dalglish recalls. "I went to the first-team dressing-room door, but I couldn't bring myself to go inside. I was too shy."

Dalglish eventually got his signatures but Shankly didn't get his and so it was Jock Stein and Celtic who profited from a soon-to-be-great footballer's bashful streak. Four League titles, four Scottish cups, one League Cup, 320 appearances and 167 goals later, Dalglish had itchy feet and wanted to test himself south of the border.

In the spring of 1977, Dalglish sat in a Chester hotel on international duty and watched the European Cup Final. "It surprised me that a number of the Scotland squad who were playing in England wanted Liverpool to lose," Dalglish recalls. "That told me that Liverpool were the team every English club wanted to beat, which aroused even greater respect."

That night, Kevin Keegan ran the German international Berti Vogts into the ground but it was his last act in red before his move to Hamburg. A replacement was needed and he'd better be good.

Birmingham's Trevor Francis and Arsenal's Liam Brady were both linked to a move but Paisley only ever had eyes for one player. He wanted Dalglish. Stein was resigned to losing his man and despite both Crystal Palace and Manchester United showing an interest, Paisley was too cute and too cash-rich to miss out.

Armed with the £500,000 the club had received for Keegan, Paisley and club chairman John Smith drove to Glasgow and returned with a new icon, and – amazingly – £60,000 in change!

"In an attempt to avoid recognition and keep things quiet, we booked onto a Glasgow hotel as brothers under the names John and Bill Smith," said Paisley. "A few minutes after we checked in, a lad came up to me and asked; "Can I have your autograph, Mr. Paisley?" Our cover had been blown." They moved quickly and within ten minutes of meeting Dalglish at Parkhead, the deal was done.

Some pundits thought the fee excessive. It was a British record but the chairman was adamant. "The best bit of business we've ever done," John Smith said at the time. Despite money in the bank, Stein had only one line for reporters: "Now where do I find another player like Dalglish?"

Bill Shankly empathised with his fellow Scot, saying, "I understand that like Kevin Keegan, Dalglish wants to get on but I would have moved heaven and earth to keep him. I would rather have quit and got out of the game altogether than sold a player of his brilliance."

Shankly greeted Dalglish on his arrival in the city and had two bits of advice, "Don't over-eat in the hotel and don't lose your accent." It's unclear if Dalglish ever over-did it at the buffet but he certainly never lost that accent.

In fact, a few years later when Avi Cohen arrived at Anfield and sat next to Dalglish at training, the Israeli international said to him, "Me, you. Same". "What do you mean by that?" asked a curious Dalglish. "Kenny – you, me, same – both learn English!"

On the pitch though, Liverpool fans immediately threw off the black armbands that mourned the departure of Keegan, as Dalglish – already compared to Johan Cruyff –- proved very eloquent with the ball. It took only six minutes of his league debut at Middlesbrough for Dalglish to calmly stroke the first of his 172 goals for the club and so it was to Anfield for the first glimpse of the new star.

"My Anfield debut came against Newcastle, who counted Tommy Craig amongst their number," said Dalglish. "I had grown up with Wee Tam, playing Scottish schools and Scottish youth with him. Before kick-off, I found Tam looking up at the sign that declares, 'This is Anfield'.

"How are you, Kenny?" he asked. "I'm all right, I think," I told Tam, "But you see that sign there? It's supposed to frighten the opposition. I'm terrified by it and it's my home ground.'"

Like a scared kid rocked by a caring parent though, the crowd eased Dalglish's fears and early in the second half, when the new man scored the opening goal at the Kop End, he was mobbed by his new followers.

"That was the start of the relationship between the Kop and me," he said. "It was a special relationship, hard to articulate how strong the bond was. We would share great success in England and Europe."

That's an understatement. Six league titles (as a player), three European Cups, four League Cups and a million memories, Dalglish and the fans certainly bonded, and the first cup was the epitome of that union. 65 minutes into a tight encounter with Bruges in the European Cup Final at Wembley and Dalglish, always probing, finds space in the box. In such a tight affair, these chances need to be taken and with the Bruges keeper rushing out, the temptation must have been to put his foot through it and hope for the best.

However Dalglish bides his time, waits for the keeper to fully commit before, like a golfer chipping out of a bunker, lofting it over him and into the far corner of the net. The jubilant goalscorer hurdled the advertising boards in a show of appreciation for the travelling fans in unbridled joy.

"I couldn't leap over them on the way back because the emotion made my legs weak," recalled Dalglish. "Seeing that goal go in was the greatest moment of my football life."

And what a life it was. His role in the 1978-79 side was mesmeric. Dalglish was the creative hub in a side full of both cunning and steel. Like red planets orbiting his creative sun, Liverpool that season were too much for their title competitors. The 7-0 victory over Tottenham at Anfield symbolised just how good all 11 players were but none was as instrumental or downright wonderful as Kenny Dalglish.

As the '70s became the '80s and Margaret Thatcher's Britain started to take shape, it seemed that her plans didn't include or care for Merseyside. Jobs were scarce, life was tough but on Saturday at 3pm, locals could come, thrive, cherish their team and clench a fist back at the rigours of life.

Dalglish, arms aloft, the grin as wide as the

Mersey, symbolised that happy defiance. "He gave me the best years of my life," enthused local playwright Dave Kirby. "In years to come, I can tell my grandkids that I saw Kenny Dalglish play."

79 goals in his first three seasons spoke of a supreme goal-getter but he was so much more. His vision was as if he had built in wing-mirrors, his weight of pass always perfect and his work ethic exemplary. He took the knocks, too. A hard man, Dalglish's ankles were not a pretty sight after games but he never hid, never let up and gave defenders plenty to think about.

"People often forget that the one quality great players need is courage," says Sir Alex Ferguson. "Kenny is as brave as a lion. He would take a kick from anyone and come back for more. Kenny is a man I shall always respect."

To most he was just 'Kenny', to the Kop he was 'The King' and to his teammates, thanks to Graeme Souness, he was known as 'Dog's', as in 'the dog's bollocks'!

Titles were won, at home and abroad, but in 1982, with Paisley building a new, younger team, Dalglish evolved with it, becoming less of the dynamic force in the side and more the conductor ("The creator supreme" as one commentator put it). If it was possible, he became even better.

In 1983, Dalglish curled another wonderful goal into the top corner of Ipswich Town's net. It was his 100th league goal for the club and made him the first player to score a ton of goals in both the Scottish and the English leagues.

Up front with him now was Ian Rush, and Dalglish was able to drop deep, dictate the pace of the play to suit him before unleashing the now eager and very deadly Rush. The Welshman once commented that he would often – having scored another goal – snigger at how simple it had been. "I'd laugh out of sheer amazement that after probing away at the opposition defence, how simple it had been in the end to breach them.

"Sometimes my amazement was the result of Kenny having threaded another simple but beautifully timed and weighted pass into space, that I had somehow anticipated this happening, got on the end of it, kept my cool and beaten the goalkeeper by passing the ball thorough the gap he had left between himself and the post. Occasionally I would think, 'Surely this level of football demands greater strategies to beat defences?' but as the old saying goes, 'football is a simple game'."

It was a simple game at Anfield. Dalglish won his second Footballer of the Year award in 1983 (he had previously won it in 1979) and seemed at the peak of his powers. A goal at Highbury that same year perfectly underlined both the team ethic and Dalglish's brilliant role within it.

John Motson's commentary sums it up: "They seem to find angles that other team's don't seem to appreciate. Lee... Dalglish... Lee again...Robinson... backheel to Dalglish. Surely, yes it was... it's on here... Dalglish has scored a quite magnificent goal and Liverpool prove again that there's no team better."

In that moment, fantastic internationals like Kenny Sansom and Pat Jennings had been made to look ordinary and Europe's top clubs must have been alerted to a player regarded as one of the world's best.

But Dalglish was never tempted to move abroad. Liam Brady, Ray Wilkins and soon Souness were all tempted by the Italian game and its lira but Dalglish wasn't interested. "I was perfectly happy where I was. I spent enough time in Europe with Liverpool."

So, he may not have felt compelled to follow others to Spain, Italy or Germany but those who hailed from those nations had certainly noticed him. Franz Beckenbauer, one of the all-time greats had the utmost respect. Dalglish was after all, King to his Kaiser. "He is one of the best players I have ever seen," gushed Beckenbauer, "and one of the best players in the history of football."

In 1984, Liverpool marched on Rome. The path was treacherous as apart from the first round, they were drawn at Anfield first and each away trip was far from easy. The Spanish champions Athletic Bilbao, their Portuguese counterparts Benfica and the Romanian heavyweights Dinamo Bucharest were all beaten in their own backyards and in the final, famously, so were Roma.

Now playing under Joe Fagan, Liverpool were perfect on the road. They had long known how to silence a crowd baying for blood but much was due to Dalglish's role. His attacking instincts would never fade but away from home against the continent's best, he was pivotal in a flexible and ingenious system. Lose the ball and there was Dalglish making up the numbers; counter-attack and there he was pulling the strings.

"We were playing a 4-4-1-1 formation with myself upfront and Kenny in 'the hole'", recalls Rush. "Kenny was superb at this because he possessed the brains, the skill and the know-how to be the conduit of the team. He was the hub around which everything revolved and, of course, when we were on the attack, his experience was of great benefit to me."

Yes, his experience. A year after Rome and in the awful wake of the Heysel disaster, Fagan retired from the game and the Liverpool board appointed Dalglish as the new player-manager. Seventeen years and countless memories after his debut as a baby-faced hopeful at Celtic, Dalglish was the boss. Unfortunately for those hoping to challenge the team for honours, he was also still the player.

He had intermittently dropped himself for two-thirds of the 1985-86 season but after a home defeat to Everton in February things looked bleak and so he threw off the tracksuit, put on his famous Puma Kings and helped the team go on one of those unbeaten runs that, well, win Championships.

The last game was at Chelsea; Liverpool needed to win and needed inspiration. It came from their manager.

A melee outside the box saw the ball hooked over the Chelsea back-four to Dalglish. Lesser players might have rushed it but Dalglish with seemingly no consideration for the implications of the day, calmly took it on his chest and placed a volley into the far corner. The arms are aloft, the smile is beaming: it means the title is coming back to L4.

A week later the Double (Liverpool's first) was won and those fans travelling back to Liverpool who thought they'd seen it all from Dalglish the player, now had a manager about whom they would talk in the same breath as Shankly and Paisley.

His appearances on the pitch were now scarce and it seemed only right that it should be he who should find a replacement for himself. Anyone else might have found the task too daunting. And then came Hillsborough.

The role of Dalglish in those dark days cannot be overstated and it was far more important, more vital, than anything that individuals might do with a football. Dalglish and his wife Marina were there for the relatives of those who lost their lives, for those who were traumatised by the day and its aftermath; they were there for a city in mourning and while it took its toll on the man, his actions will – like those who died – never be forgotten.

Dalglish resigned in 1991 and, of course, came back to the helm in 2011 for one more, less distinguished season. He must have been so disappointed to be asked to leave but he talked only of what was best for the club, one that he so achingly loves.

He got to manage Steven Gerrard though. The captain who as a boy had been asked... no, told, to get Dalglish's image up on his wall. Gerrard is one player who can say straight-faced that he got close to the sort of adulation afforded to the man who will always be The King.

When Gerrard talks about him though, he – like all the fans who watched him play – becomes that little boy with the poster again. As he put it: "Kenny Dalglish is a hero of mine and is the best player ever to wear a red shirt."

10 IAN RUSH

FORWARD

BY PAUL TOMKINS

Honours First Division Championship 1982, 1983, 1984, 1986, 1990; FA Cup 1986, 1989, 1992; European Cup 1984; League Cup 1981, 1982, 1983, 1984, 1995; Charity Shield 1982, 1986, 1990

In the team because... he scored 60 more goals than anyone else in Liverpool's history

Quote "The best striker I ever played with and as good, if not better, than anyone I've seen" – Kenny Dalglish

Greatest moment The 1986 FA Cup Final against Everton, scoring two goals that helped win the trophy

IT COULD HAVE all been so different. Frustrated by a lack of opportunities, in 1981 Ian Rush strode into manager Bob Paisley's office and demanded a move.

Eighteen months earlier, the young Welsh striker, then at Chester City, had turned down Liverpool's initial approach, believing that he wasn't good enough. Now it seemed that Paisley, having eventually secured the striker for £300,000 in May 1980, shared that opinion; to Rush, at least. Before he had got started, a move to Crystal Palace beckoned. Rush had yet to score a goal for Liverpool and Paisley told him that he was prepared to let him go.

It could also have been different in a much more dramatic way. At the age of five, Rush was struck down with meningitis and ended up in a coma. Two weeks were spent on the edge of life in Cottage Hospital, Flint. But this is a story of comebacks and of winning battles. Rush didn't just survive. He thrived.

Ian Rush made his Liverpool first-team debut against Ipswich in December 1980, but it was not going to be easy to break into one of the best sides in the world. It was, after all, a team destined to win its third European Cup in just five seasons.

Despite only 12 goals in the reserves during his first season at the club, Rush was called up as an injury replacement to play in the League Cup Final replay against West Ham. He hit the bar with a powerful drive and then, after a smart turn, shot narrowly wide from a tight angle. He kept his place for the first leg of the European Cup semi-final against Bayern Munich, but despite helping the

Reds reach the final – and despite a promise from Paisley of a place in the squad even if David Johnson, for whom he was deputising, was fit again – he did not make the 18-man cut.

His first season ended with seven league appearances, plus those two massive cup games. No goals scored. Liverpool were European champions, but Rush found it hard to get into celebratory mood.

The start of the 1981-82 season was when one of the club's greatest-ever love affairs almost ended before it began. Rush was deeply unhappy with Paisley, first for the European Cup final snub, and then for a paltry wage rise, despite his gaining first-team experience. To compound matters, he was back in the reserves as the new season got underway.

Rush, a shy young man, wispy of body and moustache, admits in his autobiography that he hated life at Anfield, and that, during those awkward first steps, he was not fond of the Reds' legendary manager. Having burst into Paisley's office, he was put firmly in his place.

"Your trouble is that you're frightened to think for yourself," the wily old boss told him. "As a centre-forward, your main job in the team is to score goals. But you haven't scored a single goal yet. That's why you're not playing."

Rush responded angrily, and said that there was no point staying at the club. "Are you saying you want to go?" was the manager's response. "If that's what you want, you can leave." In reply, Rush said, "You can stick your club!"

But as the young man stormed out, the manager threw down the gauntlet: he told Rush that he'd been bought to score goals, and if he could do that, he'd have a future at the club. For his part, Rush, having signed up to the passing mantra of the club, resolved to be more selfish on the pitch.

Still in the reserves, the goals did start flowing: six in five games. At the same time, the first team had started the season poorly, winning just two of the first seven matches, and were not scoring many. Having come on as a sub against Finnish minnows OPS Oulu, Rush finally broke his duck with a simple tap-in. Because of his simmering anger, he later admitted that it gave him no great joy.

A run-out in the League Cup followed, against Exeter, and this time he bagged two, the second from 30 yards and, according to the man himself, as good as any of the 343 that followed. Much to his chagrin, Paisley never offered a word of praise, but reward came in the form of a place in the starting XI against Leeds United in the league. Finally, with two Kop End goals, he was up and running.

He ended the campaign with 17 league goals from 32 appearances, and a further 13 strikes in the cups. The young Welshman was now officially a 30-goal-a-season striker. Only once in the next five seasons did he end with a total below that 30 mark, when injuries meant he missed a third of the league games. In those first six years he scored 207 goals in just 331 games. In other words, in every three games he started, he was worth two goals.

Although he claimed that his 1986-87 season was the finest of his career, with 40 goals scored as a move to Juventus loomed, it was in 1983-84 when he broke records: 47 in one season, making him the only player to have won the European Golden Boot while at Liverpool.

Incredibly, going into the 1987 League Cup final against Arsenal, Rush had bagged 201 goals, and had never been on the losing side in games in which he scored.

"It was incredible to go that long without

losing when I'd scored," he told *The Guardian* in 2007. "In the previous year's FA Cup Final against Everton they'd been 1-0 up at half-time and I equalised with about half an hour to go. Speaking to their players after the game, some of them said they knew they were going to lose when I scored. We ended up winning 3-1."

But with just a handful of games left at Liverpool, the record came to an end in April 1987. Rush scored first but Arsenal hit back with two goals form Charlie Nicholas for a 2-1 win. One week later, Liverpool went to Norwich: Rush scored his 203rd goal for the club, but once again the Reds lost.

By the mid-1980s, it was inevitable that Europe's best clubs would come calling. Here was a striker with an unbelievable goalscoring record in a major league, whose goals had helped Liverpool reach two European Cup Finals. The deal to join Juventus was tied up in 1986, but because the Italians already had the maximum of three overseas players, it was deferred for a year, by which time Michel Platini would retire. Of course, it didn't help that Rush would be joining a side losing its creative genius.

But the number nine's departure could have taken place as early as 1984. On the back of his 47-

goal season and European Cup Final victory, Napoli offered a mind-boggling £4.5m for the striker, a 50 per cent increase on the world record fee of the time.

It was two days before the transfer window closed in Italy, and Rush jumped at the chance of lucrative wages and a £1m signing-on fee. But Liverpool chairman John Smith was away in London, and refused to even discuss the matter. Napoli switched targets to Diego Maradona (a reasonable back-up plan!) and Liverpool kept Rush for another three years.

At the time, however, Rush was livid, and after missing out on a windfall beyond his wildest dreams, he soon feared for his career after picking up a knee injury in pre-season training. He recovered, but missing the first couple of months of the season, was limited to 'just' 26 goals.

He returned in October, and any fears that the knee wouldn't be the same were swept aside with a European Cup hat-trick against Benfica. So it was that in summer 1987, he joined Juventus for £3.2m.

In the end, his time in Italy was torrid. He scored seven league goals in 29 games, although Maradona was the top scorer with just 14, and

Marco van Basten, also in his first season in Italy, scored just three times in eleven games. Rush, however, was homesick, and after just a year abroad, Kenny Dalglish paid a British record £2.7m to bring the striker home.

To help cement his hero status, Rush always saved his best for Everton, the team he supported as a boy. His Welsh colleagues and close friends Neville Southall and Kevin Ratcliffe were routinely tormented, at a time when they would have got into the league's best XI.

In total Rush scored 25 derby goals. He equalled the previous record of 19, held by Dixie Dean, in 1987, with virtually his last touch against the Toffees before leaving for Juventus; six more followed after his return.

Three games stand out: a trip to Goodison in November 1982, where the 21-year-old bagged four goals against the Blues, an achievement still sung about on the Kop today. In total, Rush scored 13 at Goodison, almost twice as many as he managed against them at Anfield.

Next was the 1986 FA Cup Final, when the Reds came from a goal down to win 3-1, with the striker's second goal famously smashing into a camera placed in the back of the net.

The third occasion was the 1989 FA Cup Final, played in the aftermath of the Hillsborough disaster. Replacing John Aldridge on 73 minutes, he scored twice – his first goals as a substitute since his very first goal eight years earlier – which secured an extra-time victory.

Other memorable games include an encounter with Luton Town in 1983: before the game Rush had felt his boots were too stiff, so he threw them in the bath to loosen them up. Within five minutes of kick-off he already had two goals, and three more followed. After scoring five goals in a game for the first time in his professional career, a new pre-match ritual was born.

Later that season he scored four goals in just over 30 second-half minutes against Coventry. In between, he bagged a hat-trick at Villa Park on a frozen pitch, which included a thumping volley and, to complete the trio of strikes, a delicate lob. This was the first season of live televised league football, and people at home got a real treat. It was one of 16 Liverpool hat-tricks that Rush registered for the club.

While Everton were Rush's favourite opponents – he scored ten more against them than he managed against anyone else – his record against Manchester United provided stark contrast. By the time he had 24 goals against Everton, he'd yet to grab just one against Liverpool's other main rivals. It took 25 games, up to April 1992 to finally put one past United. And it just so happened to be a goal that ended the club's hopes of a first title in 25 years.

Overall, Rush scored a club record 346 times for Liverpool. When you score that many goals, all manner of types of finish are involved: he wasn't a great header of the ball, a long-range blaster or a specialist volleyer, but he still got plenty of those goals. In 1996, Dalglish noted that Rush's heading ability wasn't great, "and yet I can recall him scoring quite a lot of goals with his head".

But Rush did have his preferences, his trademark finishes. Primarily, his blistering pace often took him through on goal, particularly when Dalglish was supplying the pinpoint passes.

In latching onto the number seven's through-balls, Rush had the calmness of mind to find a finish. Although he frequently shot as a goalkeeper narrowed the angle, he was excellent at rounding them at speed. Rather than attempt to close-control dribble, which requires slowing down, he'd make a firm contact in pushing the ball wide.

If the goalkeeper didn't take him out – and plenty of penalties were won due to their fractional lateness – the ball would be yards clear. Rush, and the ball, were both moving at speed, but he frequently managed to catch it up, slide and slot it in from a tight angle. It was his trademark goal, though almost anything within the 18-yard box was in his armoury.

But if those one-on-ones were the most memorable Rush goals, then the one- and two-touch finishes within the area were his stock-in-trade. So many times he was in the right place at the right time, having lost his marker, to slot a simple side-foot finish into the net. He had a way of getting his first touch out of his feet, sending it to one side to enable a swift finish.

He'd often receive the ball with his back to goal, take a touch and then, in one movement, swivel and swipe the ball home. It helped that he was two-footed; unlike many of his contemporaries, he didn't need to waste time trying to get the ball onto his preferred foot. He could hit it no matter on which side it fell on.

The archetypal prolific forward is often referred to as a predator, and in Rush's case, it couldn't be more apt. There were the artful dodgers like Robbie Fowler, the creative geniuses like John Barnes and Thierry Henry, and bullish power-houses like Alan Shearer.

But Rush, according to Barnes in a 2006 interview, the best British striker he'd ever seen, was a true predator. There was something almost animalistic about him: the constant movement, the narrowing eyes, and most of all, the brutal efficiency of a strike.

He'd lurk, awaiting a slip, always on his toes, even if nothing looked on the cards. The tiniest miscontrol from a defender and the ball would be snatched. One touch, bang. His reactions were rapid. And just as predators prey on the weak and the tired, it's telling that almost 90 of his goals came in the final 15 minutes; that's a quarter of his goals in the final sixth of a game.

If there was a weakness, it came from 12 yards out. Penalties. He took, and scored, one vital one, in the 1984 European Cup Final shoot-out against Roma. But in actual games, he only took six, scoring three.

He once noted that had he been able to take them, he'd have scored 100 more goals. Out of the 89 players to have taken at least one penalty for Liverpool, he ranks 70th in terms of success rate. Contrast this with John Aldridge, the man who replaced him in 1987, and whom he eventually usurped in 1989.

Out of any player to have taken more than 15 penalties for the Reds, Aldridge ranks as number one, with a 94 per cent conversion rate. But this leads to an interesting comparison, particularly as many fans questioned Dalglish's decision to stick with Rush and sell Aldridge at the start of the Reds' last title-winning side.

In his two-and-a-half years at the club, Aldridge was especially prolific, but those 17 successful penalties skewed his true value to the side. With penalties, Aldridge's strike rate was 0.61 goals per game; highly impressive, but below Rush's rate in four of the Welshman's initial six seasons with the Reds. However, take away Aldridge's penalties and his rate drops to 0.42: as it so happens, absolutely identical to Rush's second spell at the club. With Barnes, Beardsley and, in particular, Jan Molby around to score the majority of the Reds' penalties, that side of Aldridge's game wasn't missed.

It's also worth noting that Aldridge played in an outstanding Liverpool side, but the latter part of Rush's career was spent in a relatively mediocre outfit, particularly between 1991 and 1995.

By 1991, Barnes had lost his pace, Alan Hansen had retired, and the remainder of the spine of the 1980s side were now in their 30s. Graeme Souness came in as manager and sold Peter Beardsley, the nearest thing the club had to Kenny Dalglish, and filled the side with expensive flops.

So for Rush to maintain a scoring rate that matched *sans*-penalties Aldridge's was doubly impressive. Rush was also a far better footballer, and harder worker, which highlights the wisdom of Dalglish's decision. The reinstated striker went on to score 26 'open play' goals in helping the Reds land another title in 1990.

In Dalglish's final season as manager, Rush scored 26 goals but also, according to my calculations, registered at least 13 assists (an amount usually reserved for creative midfielders who take free-kicks and corners) and was voted into the PFA Team of the Year for a fifth time.

His scoring instincts came to the fore again in 1994-95 when, at the age of 34, he notched 19 goals in all competitions for the second season running, as a foil for the prodigious Fowler. Now captain, Rush never looked jealous of his protégé, but was always happy to support him on and off the pitch.

He lifted the League Cup in 1995, but it would be the last trophy of his career. Stan Collymore soon arrived, and proved to be brilliant alongside Fowler. Rush had one season left at Liverpool, bagging five goals in 20 appearances, before his second, and final, farewell. He moved on a free transfer to Leeds, the opponents against whom his top-level goalscoring career kicked off.

There's little doubt that Rush's first six seasons at Anfield were enough to see him into this Best XI. But there's a before and after: Rush's Liverpool career was split by that year in Italy. Seven seasons, a year at Juventus, then another eight years back on Merseyside. While the phenomenal goalscoring feats of the first stint were not matched upon his return, time in Serie A, plus a general maturing, meant that his game was more well-rounded. In time, he would become the mentor and link-striker, passing on his wisdom to a young Fowler, just as Dalglish had helped him more than a decade earlier.

So there we have it. Some players cement themselves in folklore with a legendary act, but are not in themselves legends. But no matter how you poke, prod and dissect the word 'legend' – which has grown shabby from rampant overuse – it still holds up when it comes to Ian Rush. In 100 years, people around Liverpool will still know the

name, and what it stood for. Ian Rush is a
goalscoring legend.

OTHER BEST XI PUBLICATIONS

Best XI Arsenal

Damian Hall, Kevin Whitcher,

Luke Nicoli & Andrew Mangan

Best XI Manchester United

Sam Pilger

My Best XI Liverpool
Have a go. Not so easy..

1.

2.

3.

4.

5.

6.

7.

8.

9.

10.

11.

Contact:
bestxi.co.uk
@bestxi
@calmpub

Printed in Great Britain
by Amazon